GREEN ARCHITECTURE
AND
THE AGRARIAN GARDEN

**GREEN ARCHITECTURE
AND
THE AGRARIAN GARDEN**

BARBARA STAUFFACHER SOLOMON

First published in the United States of America in 1988 by
RIZZOLI INTERNATIONAL PUBLICATIONS, INC.
300 Park Avenue South, New York, NY 10010

Copyright © 1988 Rizzoli International Publications, Inc.
Drawings copyright © 1988 Barbara Stauffacher Solomon

All rights reserved
No part of this publication may be reproduced in
any manner whatsoever without permission in writing
by Rizzoli International Publications, Inc.

Library of Congress Cataloging-in-Publication Data

Solomon, Barbara Stauffacher.
   Green architecture and the agrarian garden.
    1. Landscape architecture. 2. Gardens.
I. Title. II. Title: Green architecture and the agrarian garden.
SB472.S66   1988   712'.6   87-43262
ISBN 0-8478-0945-5
ISBN 0-8478-0907-2 (pbk.)

Designed by Barbara Stauffacher Solomon
Set in type by Rainsford Type, Ridgefield, CT
Printed and bound in Japan

Reprinted 1909

TABLE OF CONTENTS

I
PATTERNS
(11)

The Garden of Reason
(12–13)

The Pictorial Scene
(14–15)

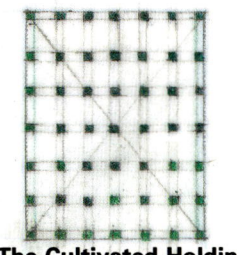
The Cultivated Holding
(16–17)

II
GARDENS
(19)

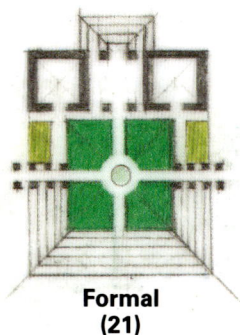
Formal
(21)

Picturesque
(31)

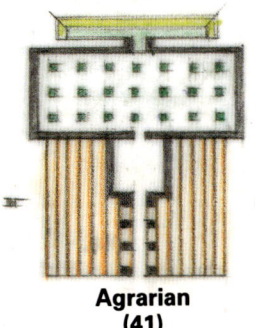
Agrarian
(41)

III
VIEWS
(51)

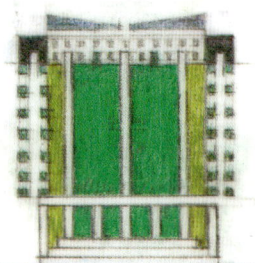
The Formal View
(57)

The Picturesque View
(69)

The Agrarian View
(87)

IV
GREEN ARCHITECTURE
(103)

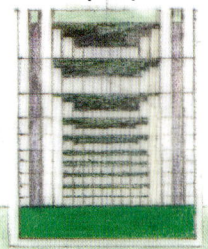
The Formal/Agrarian View
(105)

Thank you
Mildred Friedman,
Johanna Schmidlin,
David Morton,
Paula Deitz,
Paolo Polledri,
June Degnan,
Nellie, and
Dan Solomon.

**GREEN ARCHITECTURE
AND
THE AGRARIAN GARDEN**

This book is about formal, picturesque, and what I call agrarian gardens, and their relation to buildings.

Planted and built elements are arranged into formal, picturesque, and agrarian patterns in the making of gardens and landscapes. It is a convenient tactic for disclosing differences in order to view similarities.

This book was designed as it was being written. Drawings follow text, text follows drawings. A grid (in evidence, implied, or contradicted) was used from the beginning to structure the words and images on the pages. The pictorial Table of Contents and Introductions to the sections are intended to be read vertically as well as horizontally.

The small photographs and drawings are identified and credited on page **(136)**; those that are unidentified do not refer to specific sites.

LANDSCAPES
are
man-made places.

THE FORMAL GARDEN
is
the reasoned ordering of landscape with buildings.

THE PICTURESQUE GARDEN
is
a landscape of fictional scenery that consumes and trivializes the architecture.

THE AGRARIAN GARDEN
is
a cultivated holding of fields, orchards, and buildings.

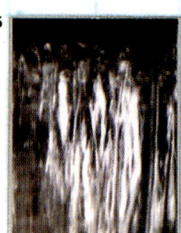

(8)

ELEMENTS
are
the simplest parts, or combinations of parts, in the landscape.

GARDENS
are
plots of landscape near buildings where herbs, flowers, and trees
are cultivated: illusions of paradise.

 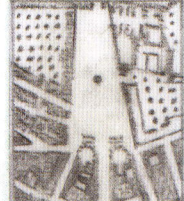

VIEWS
various and drawn,
are
landscapes and architecture, seen (or seen and not seen), talked
about, on paper, planted, or built.

GREEN ARCHITECTURE
is
where the formal and the agrarian merge, where picturesque theory
(if not patterns) is employed,
and
where architecture and landscape overlap.

(9)

I
PATTERNS

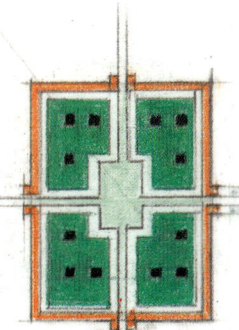

The Garden of Reason
(12–13)

The Pictorial Scene
(14–15)

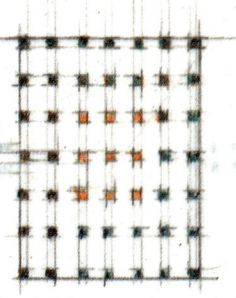

The Cultivated Holding
(16–17)

The Garden of Reason:

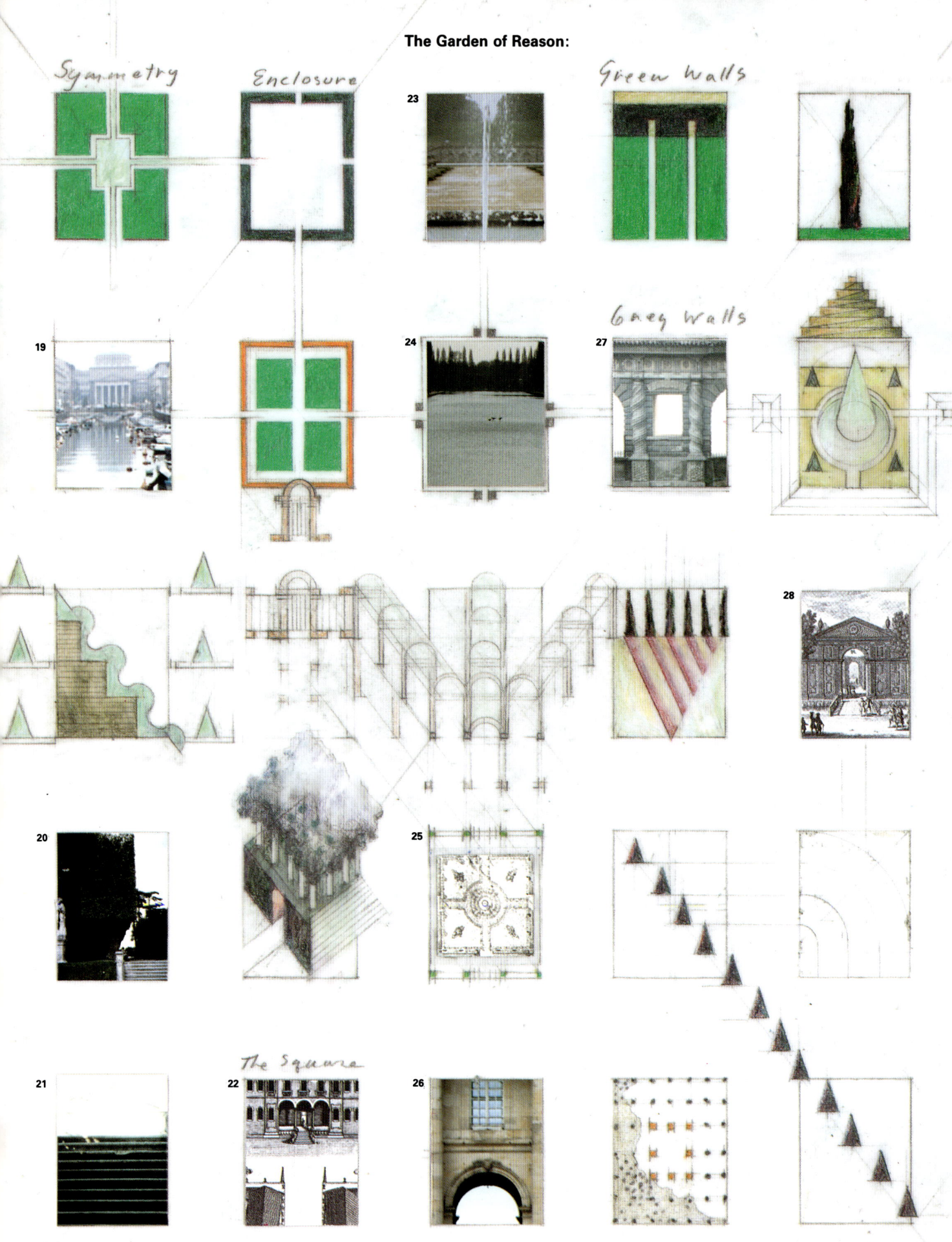

The Pictorial Scene:

Patterns of the Picturesque Garden.

(15)

The Cultivated Holding:

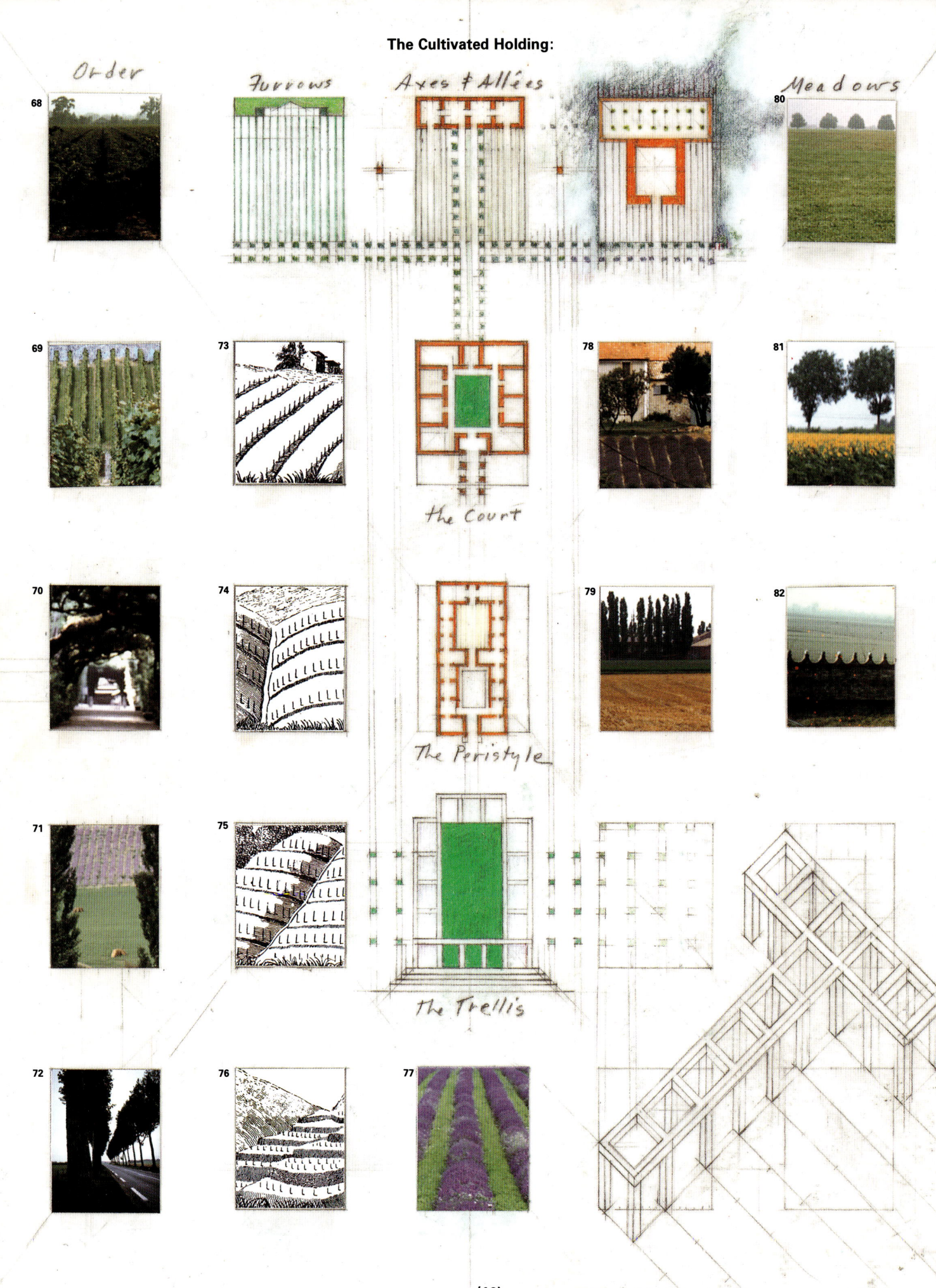

Order · Furrows · Axes & Allées · Meadows

the Court
The Peristyle
the Trellis

(16)

Patterns of the Agrarian Garden.

II
GARDENS

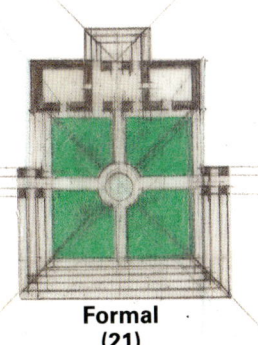
Formal
(21)

Picturesque
(31)

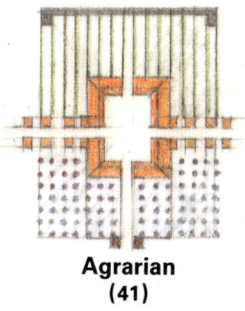
Agrarian
(41)

Villa Lante
(22–23)

Castle Howard
(32–33)

Palazzo Rossi
(42–43)

Ancy-le-Franc
(24–25)

Rousham
(34–35)

The Portico of San Luca
(44–45)

Verneuil
(26–27)

Ermenonville
(36–37)

Sonoma
(46–47)

Marly
(28–29)

Stow Lake
(38–39)

Lompoc
(48–49)

96

THE FORMAL GARDEN

Villa Lante, Ancy-le-Franc, Verneuil, and Marly are examples of gardens arranged in formal patterns.

They are ceremonial and cerebral, grand and glorious, privileged and pretentious.

"As pines keep the shape of the wind even when the wind has fled and is no longer there
So words [or walls] guard the shape of man even when man has fled and is no longer there."

George Seferis[1]

VILLA LANTE
Bagnaia

Among other events of the Italian Renaissance, the situation was ripe in 1564 to bring Mont Sant'Angelo into the form of Villa Lante. Bramante had designed the Belvedere Court at the Vatican (1520); Vignola had honed his talents in France, at Villa Giulia and at Caprarola; and the good Cardinal Ridolfi had caused an aqueduct to be built for Bagnaia (1549), and incidentally, for the Bishops' already enclosed hunting park. Tommaso Ghinucci; hydraulic engineer and architect. Giacomo da Vignola; architect and landscape design.

The villa is a place where opposites come together:

The garden of reason	+	The wilderness stageset
permanence	+	change
growth	+	decay
love of the artificial	+	love of the primitive
technology	+	arcadia
hedonism	+	righteousness
a fascination with building	+	a fascination with planting
to enjoy	+	to impress
the grotto in the ballroom	+	the salon in the forest
reality	+	fantasy
health	+	decadence
a theater for performances	+	a place to hide
geometry	+	randomness
the rational	+	the irrational

Water
descends

on axis	circuitously
through gardens parting palaces;	through salons in the forest;
from	from
the grotto Fountain of the Deluge, to	the rectangular reservoir for trout
the Fountain of the Dolphins and the chained crayfish waterstairs down to	and a jet up to the sky, the Fountain of Dragons,
the Fountain of the Giants, and the outdoor dining table with its trough for cooling wine. After that, the Fountain of Lights descends to a	the Fountain of Bacchus, the Fountain of the Unicorn, the Fountain of the Ducks, the Fountain of Acorns and
pyramid of water in a circle in a square.	The Fountain of Pegasus.

Pinewoods become
pergolas. The earth is embanked. Bright
terraces stand on dank
grottoes.
Stairways link levels.
Fountains mark landings and two identical
casinos (Palazzina and Gambara, 1568 and Palazzina Montalto, 1612)
enclose a symmetrical
fountain mountain and a hillside
green theater.

ANCY-LE-FRANC
Yonne

1545 Antoine III de Clermont-Tonnerre, owner. Sebastiano Serlio, architect.
1578 Charles Henri, Count of Tonnerre, owner.
1683 Marquis of Louvois, owner. The formal garden was replaced by a romantic lake with island and pavilion.
1844 The Marquis of Clermont-Tonnerre.
1981 Michael and Jacques Guyot, present owners.

Open daily except Tuesday, with guided tours.

Ancy-le-Franc is a pure Renaissance complex created during the Italian design invasion of France. The château, originally an island in its moat, is a square enclosing an interior court.

Each entrance to the château is centered, yet each doorway is different in design; four views of, and towards, the world are expressed.

Ancy-le-Franc was designed by Italians, but the soil is French, the trees are French. "The Italian Palace of Burgundy," Ancy-le-Franc is a French landscape.

VERNEUIL
Oise

1568 Philippe de Boulainvilliers, owner.
J.A. du Cerceau, the Elder, architect.
Jacques de Savoie, Duc de Nemours, owner.

1600 Henriette d'Entraques, mistress of Henri IV, owner.
J.A. du Cerceau, the Younger, architect.
Salomon de Brosse, architect.

Only some terraces remain.

1.
The ancient château for which the rest is a large-scale addition.

2.
Du Cerceau, writing about his work at Verneuil, puts particular emphasis on the *allées* in The Park. He refers to two in particular which Philippe de Boulainvilliers had made: One leads to the rabbit warren and the mill at the top of the hill before it circles around to the new château; the other provides *a pleasant and practical way to get from the old château to the new.*

3.
Four grand terraces of promenades and parterres, arbors and *allées*, fountains and grottoes, with a thermal bathing pavilion at the center, are surrounded by reflecting canals. Square man-made islands of garden extend into the river.

Verneuil is in that sequence of garden complexes demonstrated at Villa Lante, blown up, and out, at Versailles, and modified back to human scale at Marly.

Geometry is illusion.

MARLY
Ivelines

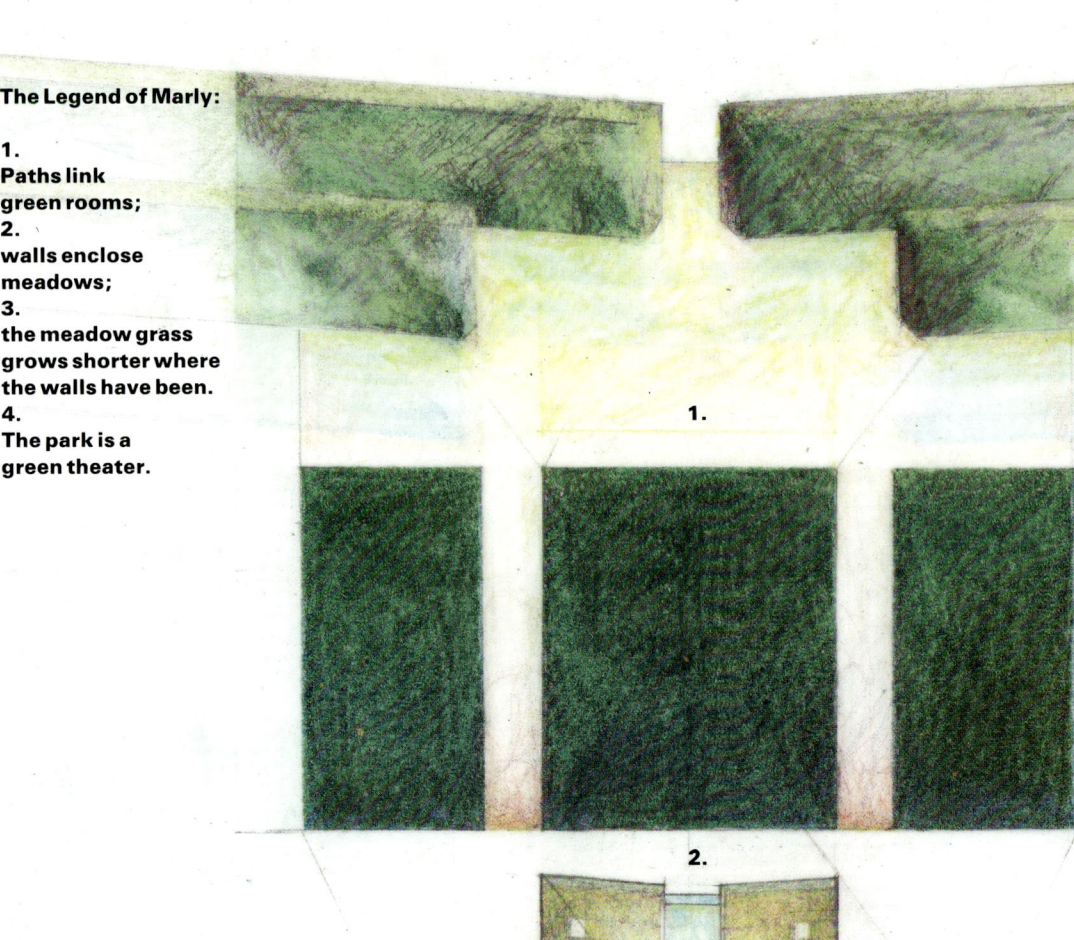

The Legend of Marly:

1. Paths link green rooms;
2. walls enclose meadows;
3. the meadow grass grows shorter where the walls have been.
4. The park is a green theater.

1677 to 1714 Louis XIV, owner and landscape designer. Hardouin-Mansart, architect.

Marly is green architecture.

Louis XIV's program called for *bosquets*. *Bosquets* enclosed green rooms. Each green room was a paradise and landEscape.

Marly was a model for its own destruction. This suburb of gilded gazebos anticipated the minimal house and recreational garden.

Today only the landscape remains. The planted forests are green walls enclosing fields for picnics.

97

98

99

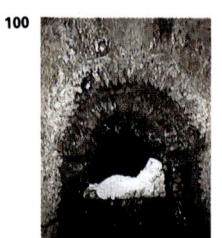

100

101

THE PICTURESQUE GARDEN

Rousham, Castle Howard, Ermenonville, and Stow Lake are gardens arranged in picturesque patterns.

They are landscapes as scenery: introspective and circuitous, melancholy and moral, narrative and romantic.

"The God of the 17th century, like its gardeners, always geometrized; The God of Romanticism was one in whose universe things grew wild and without trimming and in all the rich diversity of their natural shapes. The preference for irregularity, the aversion to that which is wholly intellectualized, the yearning for *échappées* into misty distances—these were eventually to invade the intellectual life of Europe at all points."[2]
Arthur O. Lovejoy

The internal landscape of the romantic imagination (Milton's promise of "a paradise within") accompanied autobiographical scenes in the garden. Discovering one's soul in wild nature prescribed designing gardens that pretended to be natural.

From a few private grottoes in Renaissance gardens and *folies* on pastoral farms, this persistant picture making became the correct way to design parks and parkways, golf courses and gardens, cemeteries and public landscapes.

CASTLE HOWARD
North Yorkshire

Two temples in a meadow. A *folie* in the fields.

"In the creative arts that were decisively affected by the picturesque, Vanbrugh stands out as the original innovator" when he substituted the ha-ha for the fence in order to conceive gardens as "painted landscape, with lakes, vistas, temples, and woods worked into a composed whole."[3]

Stephen Switzer advocated a style of gardening based on the connections between the classical agrarian poetry of Virgil and Pliny and the modern agricultural politics of English empiricism. He idealized the harmony between agriculture, poetry, and politics in Augustan Rome; he delighted in the landscape engineering of modern Italy. Aware that the French were revising classical (pastoral) gardening, he thought that the English should make a better job of it than " '*France* our great Competitor' in garden arts as in arms: 'Tis then we shall hope to excel the so much boasted Gardens of *France*.' " British noblemen could construct houses and gardens vying with Versailles in scale, but based on an English political philosophy which opposed "Arbitrary and Despotick Power."[4]

Five straight miles of beech and lime *allée* from Hawksmoor's Carrmire Gate and Vanbrugh and Garrett's Gate House to the 100 ft. obelisk announce Castle Howard, then turn east to the house. George London had originally intended to extend Henderskelf Lane straight into Wray Wood. When Switzer took over as landscape designer, he encouraged Lord Carlisle to retain the serpentine path around the Wood and merely decorate the grove with waterworks, statues, and winding paths.

By curving the avenue around Wray Wood this small beech-covered hill became "historic ground, since it became the turning point of garden design not only at Castle Howard but in England."[5] He might have added "and the world."[6]

Henderskelfe Castle partially destroyed by fire.
Charles Howard, 3rd Earl of Carlisle, owner, commissions new design by: Sir John Vanbrugh, stage designer, architect, and landscape designer; Nicholas Hawksmoor, architect; and George London, landscape advisor.
Stephen Switzer, landscape theorist and designer: *The Nobleman, Gentleman, and Gardener's Recreation* (1715), *Rural Gardening* (1718).
Vanbrugh's Temple of the Four Winds built. South Lake and statued terrace designed.
Hawksmoor's Mausoleum built.
Daniel Garrett's New River Bridge constructed.
Walled garden expanded to 11 acres.
The Great Lake, north of house, constructed.
W. A. Nesfield's green rooms of lawn and yew hedges, and fountain, begun.
House and grounds opened to public.
Wray Woods, felled during the war, replanted. Shrub and wild garden in Temple Hole added.

Still in the Carlisle family, Castle Howard is open daily at 10:00.

ROUSHAM
Oxfordshire

William Kent was the practitioner of the political and literary movement around Lord Burlington's circle. While Joseph Addison voiced the Whig (echoing the Roman) position that the possession and cultivation of his land insures a man his political base, and Alexander Pope talked of elevating "All gardening to landscape painting," Kent fashioned the new (Augustan) gardens of liberty.

At Rousham he retained Bridgeman's basic plan, but avowing that "Nature abhors a strait line," he wound paths along the serpentine stream and through newly created glades and groves.

He painted "history paintings" featuring miniaturized Roman structures: the Vale of Venus celebrates the Roman goddess of Gardens and Villa Aldobrandini; the Praeneste Terrace is modelled on the Temple of Fortune at Praeneste; a copy of Scheemaker's Lion Attacking a Horse recalls a state in the Fountain of Rome at the Villa d'Este; classical statuary are scattered through the green canvases.

Beyond the Heyford Bridge on a distant ridge in the fields of Oxfordshire is Kent's "eyecather," a rusticated single gable with triple arches, seen by contemporaries as a Roman triumphal arch, and his Temple of the Mill, a cottage decorated with a facade acknowledging classical husbandry united with English agricultural activity.[7]

Temples are scattered within a grove and far onto the land. The landscape is part of the garden and the garden becomes an infinite ideal landscape.

1255	Heyford Bridge built by the monks of Eynsham Abbey over the River Cherwell.
1635	Sir Robert Dormer, owner, built Jacobean house.
1720's	Charles Bridgeman plans semi-formal garden; green theater, avenue of lawn, and *allée* from the house south through the agricultural fields.
1738	Lieutenant General James Dormer, owner, and his heir, Sir Clement Cottrell, become friends of Lord Burlington.
1739–41	William Kent hired to add south facade, wings, stable block, and to redesign the garden.
1876	St. Aubyn, architect, adds north facade.
1987	Charles and Angela Cottrell-Dormer, owners, breed Longhorn cattle and maintain Kent garden.

Garden open everyday 10:00 – 4:30.

Rousham Park is a "unique document of garden art: the earliest surviving ancestor of all the landscape gardens and parks in the world."
Christopher Hussey.

ERMENONVILLE
Grand Environs de Paris

The Marquis de Girardin was a wealthy amateur interested in social and cultural reform. Cottages for agricultural workers, a model farm for agricultural experiments, and a grange for peasant festivities were constructed.

The structures were designed around Girardin's theories of a regional/vernacular style. Vernacular seems to imply a predilection for Italianate. For the 18th century French traveler, the Italian rural architecture, in its picturesque setting, represented a universal architectural style for utilitarian structures everywhere.[8]

Morel's treatise lays out four "genres" for gardens: the Poetic, which "takes its subjects from Mythology and ancient fables and sets out to present us either with an incident from the Golden Age or some pagan mystery"; the Romantic, which aims to represent "everything that the imagination can conceive and art can execute ...enchantments, fairy dreams, the wonders of magic...the most extravagant inventions...unknown to everyone except to him who conceived them or to whom the inventor takes the trouble to explain them"; the Pastoral, bucolic scenes nearer to nature; and, the Imitative "where the Artist seeks to represent a foreign country, to recreate on the terrain entrusted to him the customs, forms, products and constructions of another country or century."[9]

Girardin was concerned with the "pictures" he created from the nature he found. The view south of the château was as an Italianate Claude Lorrain; the view north, pastoral and melancholy. Another view was in the style of Hubert Robert, another in the taste of Salvator Rosa, another, recalling Jacob van Ruysdael. Literary and philosophical inscriptions clue in visitor's preceptions. A monument to modern philosophy is deliberately unfinished; it is "imperfect like philosophy itself." A catacomb is intended to remind the visitor to meditate on death. A simple hermitage might have been a criticism of the duplication of peasants' rustic huts used hypocritically for fashionable amusements and entertaining.

1762 Marquis de Girardin acquired property.
1765 Girardin (with Hubert Robert) plans estate. J. M. Morel, technical consultant and architect of individual structures.
1776 J. M. Morel: *Théorie des jardins*.
1777 Girardin: *De la Compositions des Paysages*.
1778 Jean Jacques Rousseau's tomb placed on the Isle of Poplars at Rousseau's request; Hubert Robert and J. P. Lesueru, designers.

The town hosts visitors to the Forest of Ermenonville and the *Mer de Sable*. Access to the Isle of Poplars and park is through the campsite.

STRAWBERRY ISLAND/ STOW LAKE Golden Gate Park, San Francisco	A man-made lake encloses a man-made mountain/island.	The persistent picturesque traveled to the Far West.	A park in the Olmsteadian tradition was designed onto the grid of an American city.	Elements of the picturesque garden used in the making of Stow Lake:

1883 Strawberry Lake reservoir built with Strawberry Island in its center.

1891 Sweeney Observatory built on crest of island (425 feet above sea level); Perry & Hamilton, architects.

1892 North bridge constructed.

1893 Lake renamed for Park Commissioner Stow. Huntington Falls donated by railway magnate C. P. Huntington.

1906 Observatory destroyed by April 16th earthquake.

1974 Huntington Falls rebuilt by Bond Act. Chinese Pavilion donated by Sister City, Taipei, Taiwan.

Boathouse and refreshment stand closed on Mondays.

A grid was drawn on the sand dunes of San Francisco.

The people of the city decided that a rectangle in this grid be green.

1.
an island,

2.
a serpentine lake,

3.
meandering paths,

4.
a Chinese pavilion,

5.
a man-made waterfall,

6.
a rustic bridge,

7.
a ruin,

8.
trees seemingly in natural array,

9.
grasses and man-made rocks at the water's edge,

10.
felled trees left as wilderness decor,

11.
palms mixed with cypress from the forest primeval,

12.
small overgrown islands as wildlife sanctuaries,

13.
particularly appealing ducks, and

14.
a boathouse with rowboats for rent: Paradise.

107

THE AGRARIAN GARDEN

The complex called Palazzo Rossi, the Portico of San Luca, and the California towns of Sonoma and Lompoc, are examples of landscapes arranged in agrarian patterns.

Agrarian gardens, rural and urban, are eternal (if ignored as ignoble), constant and seasonal, utilitarian and splendid.

PALAZZO ROSSI
Pontecchio
Comme di Sasso
Marconi (BO)

Legend:

1450's:
1. Canal,
2. village courtyard,
3. palace court,
4. mill, and
5. meadow.

1980's:
6. Trattoria,
7. parking courtyard,
8. fishing,
9. barn,
10. soccer field (proposed),
11. palace garden, and
12. site of annual fair.

The Rossi landlords changed the course of the river and built an urban environment as a condition to live in the countryside. The palace architecture is typical Renaissance Gothic with decorative crenellation. The integration of residence and production continues today. The palace/village is a kind of perimeter block around a central courtyard. Private residence, restaurant/store, farm, and 30 working class apartments are integrated into one rural/urban complex.

1450 Iniziato da Bartolomeo Rossi, owner, plans palace/ *borgo* (village)/ industrial complex with paper mill, lumber mill, and stables on canal channeled from the river Reno.
1482 Nestore and Mino Rossi, owner, complete plans.
1527 Bourbon troops damage complex.
1673 September 8th; first of annual *Fiera dei Setacci* (produce fair) on meadow contiguous to palace facade.
1750 Lodovico Rossi, owner, restores complex.
1773 Camillo Rossi, owner, removes tower in the interest of symmetry.
1907 Duke Gianguigi Bevilacqua, owner; restoration by Alfonso Rubbiani.
1937 Trattoria del Castello di Calzolari Ernesto opened.

Palace private. Fair continues annually. Restaurant open daily except Mondays.

In 1500 the Bolognese humanist Filippo Beroaldo noted the abundance of fresh water and the good fishing in the canal.
In 1560 Pope Giulio II honored the gardener Pietro dalla Gatta for his ingenuity, "though a peasant, a man of great creativity."[10]

**THE PORTICO OF
SAN LUCA
Bologna**

1674   A portico was extended from Porta Saragozza in Bologna to the 11th century Santuario della Madonna di San Luca located on Mt. della Guardia, three and one-half kilometers from the city.

1718   The Senate and Cardinal Origo Legato commission a portico to the pilgrimage church. Carlo Francesco Dotti, architect.

1723   Dotti built the Arco del Meloncello at the end of Bologna's urban arcade and continued the arcaded portico up the hill to the new pilgrimage sanctuary.

In daily use.

The Portico of San Luca is an example of a landscape that combines formal and agrarian elements:

There are:

1.
a long formal *portico* (porch) connecting an urban center with a holy mountain;

2.
a landscape where the distinction between planted and built elements is eliminated, and the use of permanent or impermanent materials does not define separate disciplines (garden design vs. architecture);

3.
A system of 666 almost identical elements adapted to an always varying terrain;

4.
a sequence of seemingly endless, idealized passages broken to allow a utility road up to the mountain;

5.
a monument of rendered masonry, not of precious materials;

6.
a public civic/sacred element financed by private families, each paying for their arch;

7.
an extension of the church to the city and of the city to the hills for public processions or private strolling, running, talking, sitting, playing, praying, and playacting;

8.
a pink colonnade wall viewed from across the valley, a yellow passageway with doors and windows to view the valley and to walk onto the land;

9.
a promenade open to the vistas and closed to the rain;

10.
a passage to the orchards or to the church;

11.
order, enclosure and magic;

12.
green architecture.

SONOMA
California

1542	Land claimed by the Spanish.
1573	*Law of the Indies*: Spanish Colonial laws for town planning.
1823	Land claimed by the Republic of Mexico. Mission of San Francisco Solano constructed. Vineyards planted.
1835	Mission secularized into presidio. Town planned according to *Laws of the Indies*.
1840	Mexican painter Augustin Davila prepares first map with plaza and grids.
1846	Bear Flag Revolt to make a California Free Republic.
1847	W. B. Ide shifts grid slightly.
1850	J. O'Farrell makes 20 square miles of lot numbers with their boundaries.
1862	Haraszthy introduces Zinfandel grape.
1873	Phyloxera insects plague vineyards.
1880	Italian-Americans introduce root resistant to phyloxera.

The plaza was the center of the pueblo and remains the center of the town today.

Sonoma is the Indian word for *Valley of the Moon*.

The original settlers intended a Jeffersonian community of small landowners.

The Sonoma Slough provided a major waterway from San Francisco Bay to Sonoma.

The Plaza is enclosed by adobe structures from the Mexican era, western-style wooden false fronts, and rusticated basalt structures built by Italian masons. The City Hall has identical facades facing four directions.

Sonoma is a prosperous American town that missed most of the twentieth century's tampering with tradition. It has a formal setting that induces public life, tree lined streets extending to the agrarian fields and vineyards of Sonoma County, and a monument in its Mission. It is urban and suburban, public and private, formal and agrarian.

MAP OF SONOMA 1850

LOMPOC
Santa Barbara County California

1769 Gaspar de Portola's expedition camped at Surf. Chumah Indians in residence inland.

1787 Mission La Concepcion Purisia de Maria founded.

1812 Mission destroyed by earthquake, then rebuilt, subsequently destroyed and rebuilt.

1874 Lompoc incorporated as a Temperance County by W. W. Broughton and W. W. Hollister.

1890 First flower seed farm established: W. Atlee Burpee Seed Company.

1900 Bodger Seeds established.

1930 Denholm Seeds established.

Lompoc is a gridded town on the Pacific coast of California. The grids continue from the mountains to the Pacific and are planted with flower fields.

In 1910, horticulturalist Luther Burbank (cousin of W. Atlee Burpee) commended the "mountain alluvial soil," the climate and the proximity to the sea of Lompoc Valley as a place for growing seeds.

Citizens look with delight, farmers with pride, and tourists with wonder at these rows and rectangles of flowers.

III
VIEWS

Various, and drawn,
(53)

The Formal View
(57)

The Picturesque View
(69)

The Agrarian View
(87)

The Black Line
(84)

(51)

Winter in the Veneto from Maser towards the S...

VIEWS: VARIOUS

There are:

the formal view, where the landscape and the architecture are seen with the same glance;

the picturesque (modern) view, where the landscape is filtered through one set of ideas (intuitive), and the architecture another set (intellectual);

the agrarian view, where the landscape and the architecture grow from a cultivation of the familiar.

There are:

the view drawn on the 8½" × 11" page;

the view in the photograph or in the collage of juxtaposed images;

the view on the plan or map, or from the legal document, of what is known;

the point of view of the person who sees what is in front of his eyes, and of the person who does not see what is in front of his eyes;

the near view where the front door meets the garden path;

the far view of the valley from the upstairs window;

the long view from across the valley, or written in the book, and the dissolving views of landscapes and cities always changing.

There are views *of* and *about*, *from* and *around*, *over* and *into*;

there are popular, bigoted, and academic views.

There are:

the invisible geology inside the landscape;

the "depth of invisibility" through mists and mountains; and

the problem of drawing the invisible on a piece of paper.

the problem of drawing the invisible on a piece of paper.

VIEWS: DRAWN

A drawing is different from being there; a photograph is just as different.

A drawing can try to show a place as the architect and original owner conceived it, what historians have written about it, plus the way it felt to walk through it in the rain last Sunday.

A drawing represents what is, and analyzes what might have been and could be.

A drawing can try to show a building from the inside out; what is known about it and what can not be seen. The sky and mountains are inside the front door; the bottle in the cellar is opened on the roofdeck. A drawing can try to see the building from the inside stairway to the tower view, and from the dank grotto to the glaring terrace.

To draw the common ground between an object and the landscape on a piece of paper is to draw, not the contrived shadows of architectural drawing convention, but the plan, the elevations, sections, and paths of movement. In elevation the shapes of trees change (as when one goes between Switzerland and France); in plan, cultivation is geometric. There are overlays from maps, texts, photos, sketches and memory. There is what has been read and thought.

When the "Academy of Abstraction" and the Modern movement(s) ruled, ambiguity was avoidable. Content in painting, history in architecture, and architectural drawings were out. When the architect drew, he knew that his drawing was of minor value compared to the functioning building. (Regardless, Picasso, Klee, de Chirico, and Matisse were concerned with content, and Schinkel, Le Corbusier, Frank Lloyd Wright, and Louis Kahn did not throw away their drawings.)

Modernism (and two World Wars) may have been needed to clear out history, for museums and cities to make room for pure forms and white walls, but everything became so clean it disappeared. The isolated high points that rose in this thin air barely nodded to each other.

To draw green architecture is to draw tradition back on the page. The story is told by walking from one room, indoors or out, to the next. Floors, walls, and ceilings of verdure alternate with those of stone, wood, and water. One walks through a succession of elements linked by straight lines and straight intentions. Paths radiate. Views emerge. Rows of trees color the way. One sees ahead and through transparent walls: layers. One is not lost. Stairways and ramps allow the players to move through space rather than stare at it. The action involves remembering old texts and where you were five minutes ago. The story is not revealed at any one point; there is surprise and ambiguity. But if one wants to go someplace, one can see a way to get there.

THE FORMAL VIEW

the Western formal garden came from the paradise garden of Persia, to be perfected in France. From there it became a symbol of aristocracy and authority, to many people an anathema.

The rich man owns a garden; the poor man works it.

THE FORMAL VIEW

113

The formal garden is as man-made as its juxtaposing architecture. It is the work of our hands, an artificial homeland. God and Adam were gardeners.

The garden of reason is an orderly representation of paradise. Xenophon's (ca. 400 B.C.) description of a pleasure garden notes "The beauty of the trees, the accuracy of the spacing, the straightness of the angles, and the multitude of the sweet scents."

Homer describes the gardens of Alcinous as four acres of enclosed gardens with fruit trees and vineyards in straight rows surrounded by a green hedge.

The paradise garden traveled with the Arabs to Spain, to Italy and to France. It was an ordered and enclosed place, a green rectangle divided by water (or a path) into four quarters of equal size. Sometimes an island (the unattainable) was placed in a central pool of water.

This formal pattern accommodated to different terrains and temperaments. In each country it had antecedents in local farm gardens. The ground plans grew into different vertical elements and elevations in the hands of people with different views.

The architectural character of European gardens predates the influence from the Near East. Proto-historical fields are rectangular. The plains of Padua preserve remains of trees reinforcing Roman *centuriatio* gridding of the land.[11]

In Spain most cultivation consists of grids of olive orchards covering the plains and crammed onto terraces retained by dry stone walls. The dry earth (*secanos*) contrasts with the irrigated zones (*regadios*). These paradise gardens reflected Arab, then French and Italian, patterns of arranging built and planted elements. Anything green was rare. Water and shade were precious.

A garden was an island. Water, running down, jetting up, reflecting the sky or black cypress, became a garden. The square courts of farm complexes centered on a well; the life of urban plazas revolved around fountains; the smallest patio proudly held a potted plant.

114

Italy, varied and lush, was resplendent in contrasts. In Italy, buildings, gardens, and agriculture merge. Layered views link one with the other. Hills provide the Italians the delight of moving earth, making terraces promenading on embankments and enjoying the view. In the thirteenth century, horizontal furrows reshaped the landscape of many hills. Terraces of earth were transformed into terraces of marble. Stairways link levels. Furrows lead to columns. Rows of trees become colonnades. Walls and field houses connect to become villas. Grids of orchards become ground plants for temples. Green walls alternate with walls of masonry. Inhabited nature is the garden and the farm. Arbors and colonnades are green architecture.

Tuscan and Roman history was expressed in a desire to manipulate nature through predetermined elements and patterns. Classicism prescribed symmetry, rules of proportion and a geometry that occasionally degenerated into decoration. Allegorical programs called for pagan gods to romp in the gardens of Christians. Pastoral settings alternated with artificial tricks. Human nature was expressed in subjective displays, surprising topiaries, and water jokes. Gardens were a transition from fantasy to the real world (or, landscape, an immediate refuge from it).

When, around 1342–45, Boccaccio describes his first garden in Naples, it is a garden laid out by the French.

France, open and green, allowed the French to express their proclivity for clarity and broad horizons. They expanded the paradise plan and added monumental simplicity and grandeur.

Aspects of thirteenth and fourteenth century French culture (chivalry, love poetry, secular music, mathematics, mechanics, various philosophical ideas) reflect Near Eastern influences. So also do elements of concurrent gardens (the symbolic imitation of the Garden of Eden with its four rivulets, ordered geometrical patterns, the special use of water, and the planting of vineyards interlaced with roses). Syrian roses and Islamic grapes were imported. Covered allées, porticos, greenhouses, musical fountains, and Houses of Daedalus (labyrinths) were built.[12] For the French, building a garden has always meant making green architecture.

In the formal view, **order** is orientation, not alienation:

An orchard is an ordered garden. To order a garden is to follow the patterns of the gods. Cultivation is geometrical.

There is solace in the clarity and illusion of order when elements relate to each other.

Straight paths bring views of the horizon. Green walls enclose meadows and shelter secret salons. Order includes variety; reason leads to fantasy. In an ordered landscape bewilderment subsides.

"To engage roses becomes a geometry."
William Carlos Williams
Spring and All in *Imaginations*

"Actually a [swimming] *pool* is, for many of us in the West, a symbol not of affluence but of order, of control over the uncontrollable. A pool is water, made available and useful, and is, as such, infinitely soothing to the Western eye."
Joan Didion
The White Album

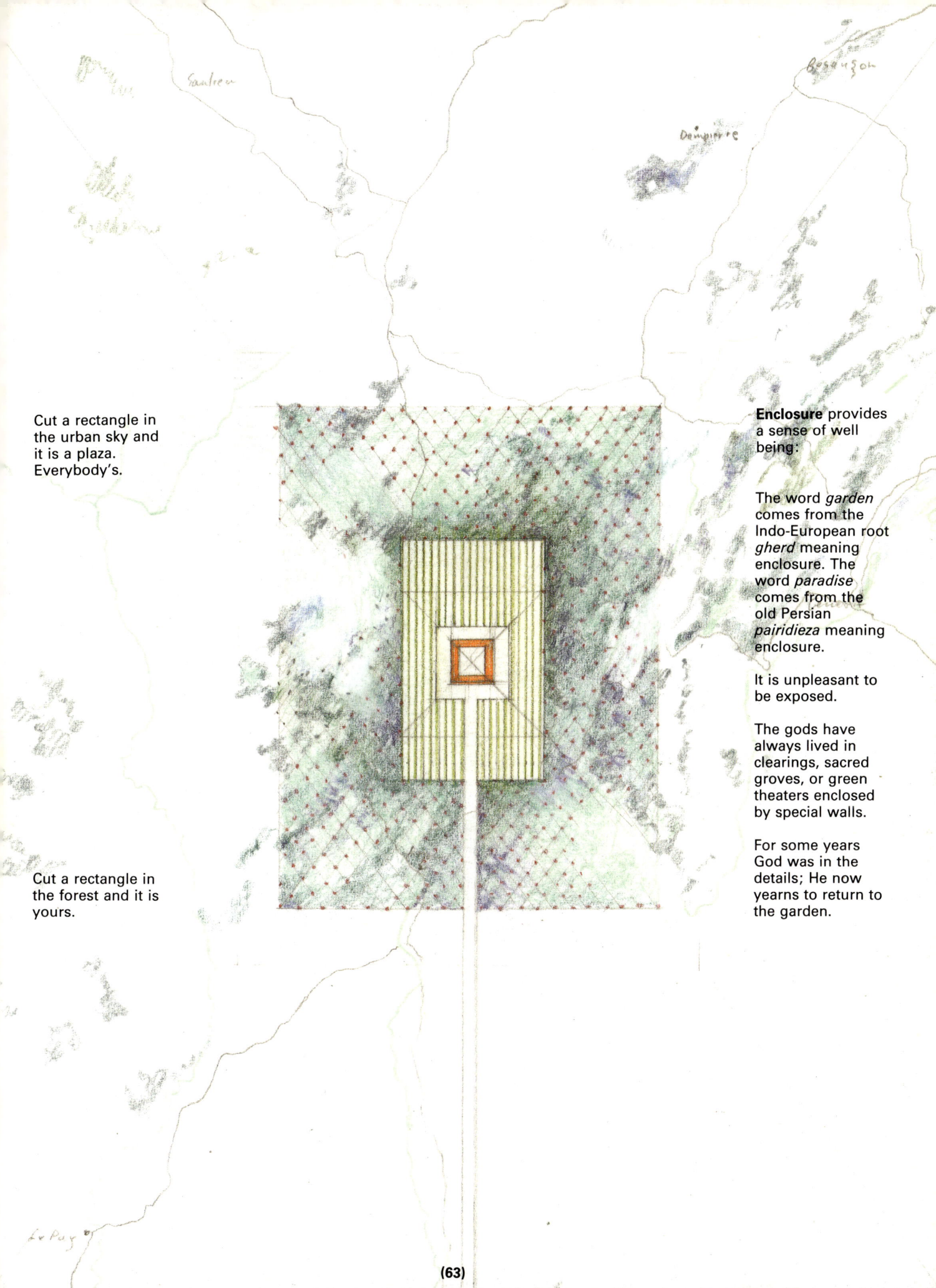

Cut a rectangle in the urban sky and it is a plaza. Everybody's.

Cut a rectangle in the forest and it is yours.

Enclosure provides a sense of well being:

The word *garden* comes from the Indo-European root *gherd* meaning enclosure. The word *paradise* comes from the old Persian *pairidieza* meaning enclosure.

It is unpleasant to be exposed.

The gods have always lived in clearings, sacred groves, or green theaters enclosed by special walls.

For some years God was in the details; He now yearns to return to the garden.

Magic includes the art of producing illusion by legerdemain. Illusion is reality.

A garden is illusion (historically, stylistically, personally).

Magic is in the line of trees that is a garden.

We plant a palm, and the palm, standing alone, or in rows, assuredly leads to paradise.

The garden exists somewhere between nature and art. The fountain/grotto/ nymphaeum are elements alluding to both. So, too, the colonnade. Or the ruin. Or a field of poppies.

Renaissance gardens, ordered and man-made, carried on their own romance with disorder. Along the paradisical riverlets and square islands of green were magic grottoes, ruins, pastorals and ornamented groves. Italians and French enjoyed their nostalgia for arcadia, their longing for escape and isolation in the garden.

There was always an irrational side of the garden of reason.

Magic is illusion. The wilderness is in the drawing room; the salon is in the forest. Torrential arrangements of rocks and waterfalls decorate the ballroom; rooms covered with mirrors, rare stones, and seashells hide in the forest.

In his formally planted garden, Pliny the Younger (ca. 100) noted that "on a sudden in the midst of the elegant regularities you are surprised with an imitation of the negligent beauties of rural nature."[13] Renaissance gardens sought this justapoxition of nature (the meadow) and art (the formal garden.)

In Italy, Alberti, suggested (1452) building caves of oyster shells and grottoes of green wax imitating moss. Complete mimesis would insure maximum surprise. In France, Bernard Palissey delighted in constructing (1563) romantic grotto walls covered by faience birds and bugs.

There is magic in the ambiguity of nature being confused with art and art with nature. Gardens provide art created from nature and nature (by man's art) created from nature. Geology produced new skills for building illusion.

There is magic in Villa Giulia's conjured roofless theater for popes and butterflies; in Verneuil's arbors encircling the hillside and lap pools forming green islands. There is magic in Villa Lante's sacred grove and green theater, in Villa Pigneto's palace for picnics, in Marly's gilded "colony of gazebos," in Rambouillet's salon of sea shells and marble grotto dairy, in the insides of outdoor theaters and the outside of movie houses, in the back of Grey Walls, in circus tents, grape arbors, cafés under trees and markets under glass, in piers for promenading straight out into the Pacific and city streets made of water.

The fantastic side of the formal garden:

GAILLON
Eure

There is magic in the island at Gaillon: a "large mountain in a small box."

1501 Cardinal Georges d'Amboise constructed château on existing foundation.
1506 Pierre de Mercogliano, garden design.
1550 Cardinal Charles de Bourbon, owner.
1565 Jacques Androuet du Cerceau, the Elder (attributed), architect.

Château destroyed. Ruins of garden remain.

Du Cerceau wrote in 1567 of this design as *A place of isolation full of pleasure;*

and, about the same time, Montaigne reacted with *Que sçais-je?*

Colin Rowe talks of this *highly assertive, slightly frenzied episode;*

John Sherman finds *a fascinating ambiguity of reality*, naturalism and idealization, illusion and reality; an artificial rock hermitage (with hermit in residence) and planted green stone rooms for dining; Eugenio Battisti finds Gaillon *Renaissance picturesque*—a legerdemain of built rock mountains with white arcadian ruins.

As Shakespeare's Touchstone put it: "The truest poetry is the most feigning."[14]

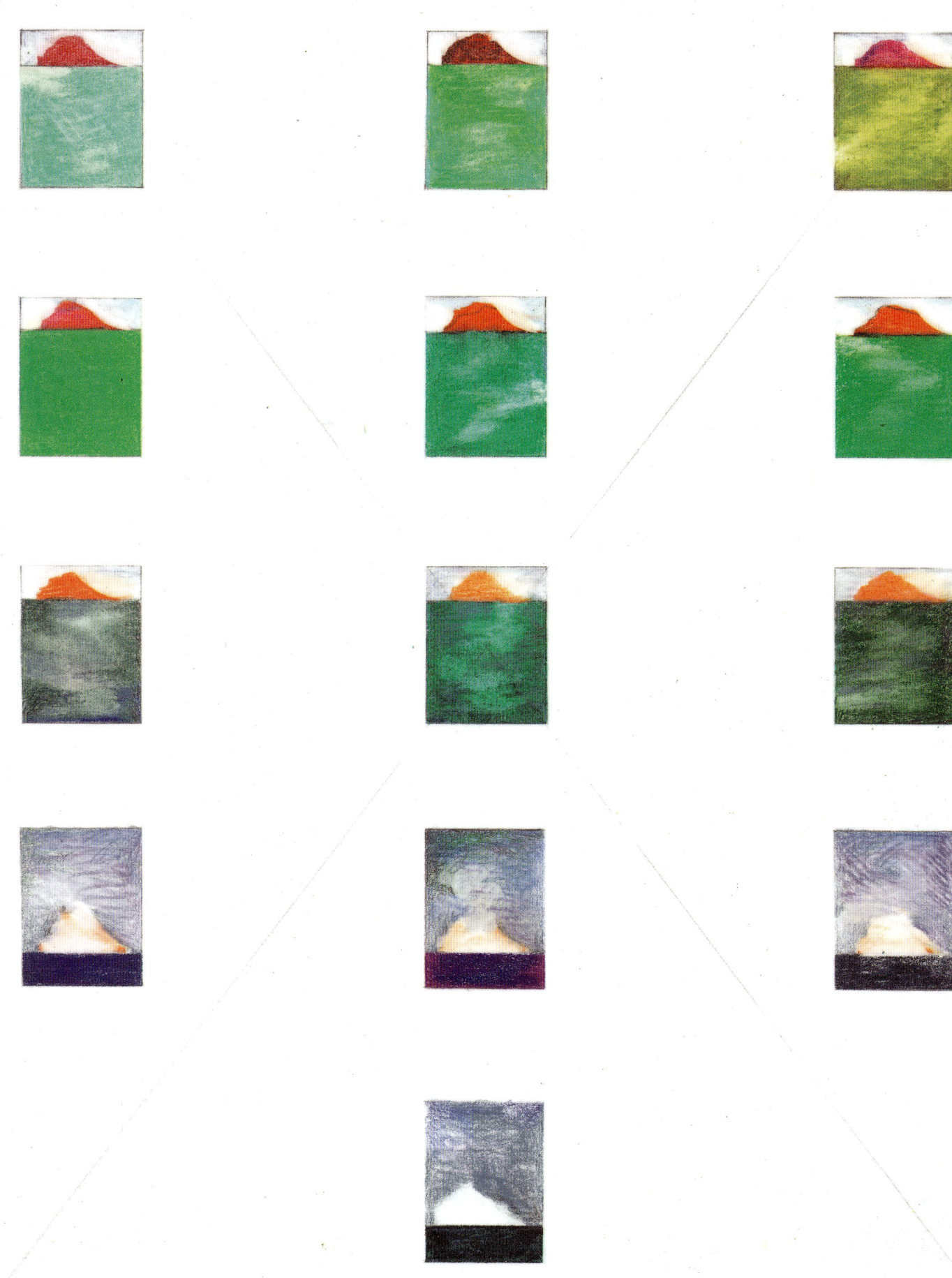

THE PICTURESQUE VIEW:

That view that came to be called picturesque is visible in the sixteenth century Italian and French "Renaissance picturesque."[15]

Giardini segreti (rather than *parchi pubblici*) conjured up the pastoral and the illusion of pleasant solitude.

Italian groves (trees planted in some order, including carefully planned disorder) and grottoes (*folies* created with architectural skills, including the ability to hide the creator's skill) produced amazement. Wildernessess decorated with the habitats of demons evoked fear.

In their pursuit of classical thoughts and pastoral images, Renaissance men were in close contact with those gods and sirens who lived in fountains, grottoes, rivers and oceans, and on magical islands.

The idea of an island—a finite world, enclosed, magical—is a seductive metaphor for the imagination. The apparition of an island is a powerful magnet for the eye. Islands are targets for conquest, mental, or visual. They are romantic and picturesque.

For the man (Richard H. Dana) who can write "There is no scenery at sea," the sight of an island on the horizon is heaven.

The island is a man-made mental heaven or hell (hell possibly fast following heaven). Here there is splendid isolation or insular loneliness.

An island is a fictional place, a place of the imagination, and as such, a paradigm for the picturesque.

There are:

Is-lands, pragmatic, yet romantic, stage sets for farms and cities;

Eye-lands, perceptual places to be seen from a distance; and

I-lands, subjective places that are thought of as desirable or dreadful (or desirable, and then dreadful).

Is-Lands:

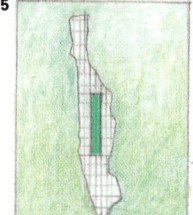

Places to be lived in.

Some islands become real cities rather than imaginary retreats. Because of their proximity to the mainland or distance from it, because of their history or despite it, because of their position on the trade routes, harbors, water supply, weather, vegetation, geological configuration, or because they willed it, they are centers of the world.

Manhattan is an island that has order, enclosure, and magic. There is order in the city's grid plan around a green rectangle of paradise. There is enclosure by the Hudson and the East River, by the Harlem River and New York Bay. In turn, urban walls enclose Central Park. Manhattan is a manmade mountain/cathedral on a rock: a real illusion.

"We'll take Manhattan.... a great big toy, just made for a girl and boy.... a summer festival.... the big apple.... New York, New York, it's a wonderful town...."

And it is a fact that Venice rose from the sea.

Eye-lands:

Places to be seen from a distance

The island is an art object to be seen, isolated, against a bare wall of sky.

Romantic islands are best seen from afar. Isolde, the unattainable. Isola Bella (built 1630–71) was to be a garden/galleon in Lago Maggiore. Never finished as intended, but never allowed to go to romantic ruin, it is best seen in drawings of how it should have been, or through a mist from across the lake.

The Isle of Poplars, tomb of J.J. Rousseau is the epitome of the picturesque island. A circle of Italian poplars and a sarcophagus stand, unapproachable and memorable, on a small island just out of reach.

"In the great atlas of imaginary geographies, the most beautiful representations are always those of the island of Utopia."[16]

The man-made mountain/island in the Paris park Butte Chaumont is an urban wilderness with a classical temple at its crest.

I-lands (of delight):

Moulin-Joli, the first picturesque garden in France, was created on three islands in the Seine.

Places that are a state of mind.

A place of the imagination, a chimerical dream.

In the Dream of Poliphilus, walls, towers, chariots, and boats were grown of boxwood on an island. Homer describes Alcinous' garden on the Island of Scheria as a paradise of vineyards, orchards, and flowers:
"On the trees fruit never fails"; in front of the vineyard "the grapes are green and shed their flower, but a second row are now just turning dark;
"trim garden-beds... all the year are gay." One fountain scatters "its streams throughout the garden"; another course[s] beneath the courtyard gate" to provide the people of the town with water.[17]

England, always fond of make-believe buildings and picture book landscapes, strove and succeeded, to a remarkable degree, to become a picturesque island/garden.

To plant or build on an island is to alter a rock in the water into a magical or menacing illusion of someplace that is not just a rock in the water.

Paradise or cemetery? Pleasure garden or exile? Memory or oblivion? Private, exclusive, beyond.

"Rien de plus agréable que l'aspect de l'île..." Bougainville.

Islands are places for islomania, islophilia,

(72)

I-lands (of desolation):

or islophobia.

THE PICTURESQUE VIEW

121

Pic·tur·esque \ :pikche:resk, -ksh- \ *adj* [modif. (influenced by¹ *picture*) of F & It; F *pittoresque,* fr. It *pittoresco,* fr. *pittore* painter (fr. L *pictor,* fr. *pictus* —past part. of *pingere* to paint— + *-or*) + *-esco* -esque—more at PAINT] 1 a : like a picture : resembling or suggesting a painted scene : suitable as a subject for painting ‹~ village› ‹~ fishing fleet› ‹discovered grouped in ~ attitudes about the stage— W.S. Gilbert› b : pleasing or charming by reason of quaintness : creating informal patterns of shape, light, and color ‹a pleasantly ~ style of architecture› ‹venerable family mansion in a highly ~ state of semidilapidation—T.L. Peacock› c : unusual, primitive, or markedly characteristic in appearance : QUAINT ‹modern touches without sacrificing its ~ French colonial charm— Mary R. Johnson› ‹pioneering conditions that are ~ to look back upon but were rather trying to live through—Marquis James› 2 : characterized by an interest in what is picturesque ‹easy for a ~ historian to lay side by side the most glaring contrasts—Virginia Woolf› 3 : evoking mental images : VIVID ‹~ epithets› ‹gave a ~ account of his adventure› —pic·tur·esque·ly *adv*— pic·tur·esque·ness *n* -ES

Every person has an occasional desire for the solace or amusements envisioned on an enchanted island. Every country has a few irrational follies in the garden.

The irrational side of the Italian and French gardens of reason, until recently ignored by (English) writers on the formal garden, anticipated the picturesque view. But, while Gaillon's "Renaissance picturesque" presented only one among many memorable French images, the English preferred to go directly to Italian sources for their landscape gardens. For the English, opposition to French politics meant opposition to French gardens. In order to compete with and surpass *La Grand Manière*, they had to devise a style antithetical to the Cartesian system of garden design.

Italy supplied variety and intricacy, classicism and naturalism, theatrical amusements and pastoral simplicities. During the Grand Tour, Rome in ruins followed the Alpine wilderness. Sir Henry Wotton wrote in 1642 that he found in Italy "a delightful confusion ... as if he had bin Magically transported into a new Garden."[18]

There was something for every fancy. There were the illusionary theatrics of Isola Bella, the cascading frenzy of Villa d'Este's fountains, the irregularity and roughness of Buontalenti's grotto at the Boboli Gardens. The *Sacro Bosco* at Bomarzo evoked wonder, confusion and terror. Villa Lante had marble gods and gleaming fountains in its green groves. Villa Giulia its stone maidens in the grotto. At Villa Mattei statues of wild boar and wolves decorated serpentine paths in the *boschetti* (groves planted in deliberate disorder) while a dragon surprised those who discovered the center of the labyrinth. (But even that symbol of confusion, the labyrinth, was enclosed in a circle or square.)

Italian theater provided elements for the new natural garden. In Vitruvius: "satyric scenes are decorated with trees, caverns, mountains, and other rustic objects delineated in landscape style."[19] Serlio illustrated this scene. His "satyric" stage designs, with rustic cottages set in landscapes, were a source for Indigo Jones and Alexander Pope, the poet who believed "Gardening more ancient and nearer to the authentic work of God than even poetry."

William Kent in 1753 proclaimed (by Horace Walpole) "the friend of nature ... the Calvin of this reformation [in gardening] ... who leaped the fence and saw that all nature was a garden,"[20] studied painting in Italy and was familiar with The Bibienas's theater sets in Rome.

A romantic craving to live in illusion allowed the garden (and then the real landscape) to imitate theatrical scenery (plus those familiar sources of the picturesque: classical literature, pastoral landscape painting, Chinese gardens, northern myths and political proclivities).

122

Each landscape garden (Manfredo Tafuri suggests we should say "*pyschologistic* garden"[21]) was a confession (more fictional than autobiographical?). Each owner represented his fantasies and prejudices in the most elaborate scenery his imagination and pocket book could produce. Ornament was superior to utility since it displayed the (castle) owner's superior aesthetic sensitivity and, by association, his wealth.

Michel Le Bris, invoking Milton's *Paradise Lost*, writes that "these gardens are never innocent: they are the interior landscapes which always record our relationship with Man, with the World and with God."[22]

Italians mixed the make-believe pastorals, the real farms and the formal gardens. While excited by the fanciful grottoes of the villa gardens, gentlemen on the Grand Tour, familiar with classical literature on rural retreats, enjoyed the georgic views vignetted by the groomed groves. The villa, the garden and the vineyards were layered in drawings and memories. This happy confusion was to be transplanted onto English (and French) soil. Memory and imagination transformed traditional farmsteads into *fermes ornées* (ornamented farms). John Dixon Hunt points out the paradox of an "English gardening that was foreign in inspiration, a new style that was ancient."[23]

What had been a mere farm was now a fantasy. "How easy then," Hunt admits, "for an Englishman with the right habit of mind to look at a piece of his own native scenery and see it as classical."[24]

Robert Castell's *The Villas of the Ancients Illustrated* (1728) helped. Castell subtly transforms Pliny's text into contemporary English ideas. The reconstructable architecture remains classical; the illusionary landscape combines an Englishman's memories of Italy with the new English landscape theories.

It is said that Philip Southcoate, owner of Woburn Farm, Surrey, was the first to decorate his estate according to "his idea of the *ferme ornée* from Fields, going from Rome to Venice."[25] Southcoate placed the ingeniously cunning ha-ha, a ditch, invisible until one almost fell into it, around his estate (hypocritically insuring the removal of the real world, workers, and workings of the farm).

Within it a circular path lead to specific points for viewing appropriate vistas. Pastoral meadows were in view; furrowed fields were outside the frame. The path was ornamented with a Gothic temple and a menagerie. This *ferme ornée* was both admired as a "blend of the useful with the agreeable" and criticized for its "profusion of ornament."[26]

ro·man·tic \ rō'mantik, -maan- -tēk *sometimes* re'- *adj* [F *romantique,* fr. obs. *romant* romance (fr, MF, fr. OF *romans, romanz* French, something composed in French, tale in verse) + *-ique* -ic—more at ROMANCE] 1 : consisting of or similar in form or content to a romance ‹my advance toward ~ composition—Sir Walter Scott› ‹~ fiction› 2 : having no basis in fact : being the product of invention or exaggeration : FABULOUS, IMAGINARY . . . 3 : impractical in conception or plan : UNREALISTIC, VISIONARY . . . 4 : marked by the imaginative or emotional appeal of the heroic, adventurous, remote, mysterious, or idealized characteristics of things, places, people . . . ‹makes a deep impression on the mind; far deeper than the less ~, everyday thing which shows the real state of an island in the statistical sense—R.A.W. Hughes› . . .

123

In 1745 William Shenstone, a poet who had never been to the Continent, created the Leasowes, Shropshire. Shenstone ("A master of the artificial-natural style in poetry": Saintsburg) was supposedly inspired for his pastoral *ferme ornée* by a type of rural gardening that was classical. According to a French critic: "it is designed for the shepherds of Guarini and of Fontanelle. There are no pastures here, no closures, no animals, nor any of the farm buildings which are included in the *genre pastorale*..."[27]

Among the elements included in this natural/English/Landskip garden were: Virgil's Grove, a Temple of Pan, a new ruin of a Gothic priory, a root house, a lead statue of a peeping Faunnus, a Latin inscription to the goddess of health, and innumerable philosophical inscriptions. Shenstone admired variety, not clarity: "So far as the imaginative reward is concerned, tedium is the result if we walk along a straight path towards an object which is already in sight. The foot should never travel to [the object] by the same path which the eye has travelled over before. Lose the object, and draw nigh obliquely...."[28]

Garden theorist Thomas Whateley approved. Emotional associations were superior to utility. The "highest" type of farm practices no functions;[29] it evoked literary pastorals. Topography was scenography.

Nature was political. Since 1721 Addison had encouraged his readers to decorate their holdings, "to make a pretty Landskip of his possessions." The shape of your trees clued the world into your political opinions. Trees should be as free as men should be from the constraints of straight lines, too many rules, and objective order.

The working farm patterned on an agricultural order was not discussed. The gentlemen landholders saw what they wanted to see.

For the English, the *ferme ornée* was a landscape composed of pictures to be viewed by the owner and his friends; for the French, the *ferme ornée* was a theatrical setting in which the owner and his friends could play the rural life.

As the name might imply, the *ferme ornée* existed in France before it appeared in England as an English "invention."[30] Traditionally, some French estates were designed to be both useful and ornamental. The *style champêtre* is evidenced in Mansart's pavilions at Marly, Le Vau's entrance to the Château of Saint-Sepulchre's agricultural estate, and the Hermitage at Fontainbleau. There are descriptions of a dairy decorated with sea shells, statues, and white marble, and a pavilion in the center of a working orchard covered with mirrors, marble, and frescoes of landscapes.[31]

124

In France outdoor pageants and garden spectacles created by Italian set designers and fountaineers, determined the forms of the garden. The sixteenth century Italian design invasion brought Serlio's treatise to the Paris theater and the Francini family of impresarios to the gardens. Charles Dufresny, the inventor of the picturesque garden in France in 1714 turned from dramatist to garden designer.

French artists traditionally made the Grand Tour to Greece and Rome. Pliny's villa was reconstructed in France in 1699, almost twenty years before Castell's folio and fourteen before Pope's praise of the gardens of Alcinous. In 1758 the French architect Julien David Leroy published his *Ruines des plus beaux monuments de la Grèce*.

The seventeenth century French habit of organized performances and private playacting in the garden was combined with the eighteenth century interest in pastoral drama and pursuit of rural retreats. The political situation made retirement to the country desirable; economic necessities made unclipped trees remarkably attractive. Social and philosophical pressures suggested that farms be useful even if they were ornamental. Agricultural experiments and Physiocratic ideals were combined with the current visual fashions on these "fields of illusion."

Whatever statues appeared in the pasture, the *ferme ornée* depended on, and was supported by, an agrarian economy.

In 1745 Claude-Henri Watelet (wealthy, an artist, interested in pastoral drama, a Physiocrat and a friend of Rousseau and Hubert Robert) returned from Italy. He purchased three islands in the Seine near Paris and created Moulin-Joli: "Usefulness will be the foundation of my art; variety, order and fitness its ornaments."[32]

On the largest island he created a formal *jardin francais* with straight allées opening to picturesque views of the countryside. He added paths and sheep, groves and green rooms, but no garden structures (*folies*). The mill was restored. A cow barn/dairy constructed. His house was a simple *maison bourgeois*. The mainland garden was traditional: Moulin-Joli was a gentleman's working farm.

Watelet's *Essai sur les jardins* (1774) was the first French treatise on the picturesque garden. He discussed the history of gardens from the natural (where gardens were made by the workers/cultivators of the land), to artificial (which he disliked as architectural and urban) to the natural-artificial (where utilitarian structures were designed to be agreeable). Watelet discussed picturesque, poetic and romantic "inventions" used to make rural gardens but advised only pastoral for the countryside. He was as opposed to English artifices as he was to the artificial in France.[33]

MOULIN-JOLI
Yuelines

1754 Claude-Henri Watelet, owner and planner of estate.
François Boucher, painter and *architecte par amitié*, remodels house.
1760 Watelet: *L'art de peintre*.
1774 Watelet: *Essai sur les jardins*.
1763 Watelet makes second trip to Rome with painter Hubert Robert.
1786 Watelet's death; estate sold.
1787 Estate destroyed.

Drawings and descriptions are all that remain.

The Abbé De Lille: "Such is the simple style where, suspending its course, the Seine, pure as your morals, free as your days, separates itself into shady canals, and secretly visits the retreat of a sage. Your art supports it; not the false art which profanes the places it pretends to adorn. Worthy to see, to love, to feel nature, you treat its beauty as a pure virgin, who blushes at her nudity, and fears adornment."[34]

The French *déterminés* found Moulin-Joli too "wild;" the Prince de Ligne recommended it for anglomaniacs.

125

folie (fo'li), *n.f.* Madness, distraction, dementia, lunacy, folly; piece of folly, foolery; extravagance, misguided passion or enthusiasm; jest, mad thing, mania, hobby; * country house for recreation. *Aimer à la folie*, to love to distraction; *dire des folies*, to talk wildly; *faire des folies*, to squander money, to behave foolishly; *faire la folie de*, to be foolish enough to; *tenir de la folie*, to be akin to madness; *un accès de folie*, a fit of madness.

Cassell's French-English English-French Dictionary (London, 1958).

Moulin-Joli, Ermenonville, Le Raincy, and Rambòuillet were, for all their owners' pleasure in picturesque views and philosophical inscriptions, working (experimental) farms. After the Peace of 1763, when the mania for everything English became fashionable, rustic huts were organized into *hameaux*. A *hameau* is a rustic hut faced with natural materials on the exterior and decorated with great luxury and fantasy on the interior.

The simple rural structures (inside and out) at Moulin-Joli and Ermenonville were transformed into simple/outside and fantastic/inside *folies*. They are pictures-of-a-house made larger, but not full size: a *hameau* was one *folie* among many scattered in the now fashionable *jardin anglo-chinois*. The georgic, if quixotic, intentions of the owners become private scenarios.

An anonymous author in 1775 (who suggested that the new gardens were inspired by poetry and the operatic decorations for Rameau's *Castor and Pollux*) describes "a country estate which has no château, but rather, twenty cottages, dispersed in a grove and with rustic exteriors and well-appointed interiors. To each cottage was joined a garden, stable, orchard, kitchen garden, parterre, trellis, espalier, and each ensemble differed from the other according to the conditions of the soil and orientation. Freedom was enjoyed by all, for each inhabitant believed himself to be the owner of his cottage and farmed his property as he pleased."[35]

The "modern hamlet" at Chantilly, a model for all later *hameaux*, consisted of a dining hall, a salon, a billard room, a reading room, a kitchen, a mill and a stable. This complex, with its kitchen garden and orchard, *rocher* and grotto, meandering paths, great lawn and water canals, was built on a number of artificial islands made by a lake and the grand canals of Le Nôtre's garden.

These huts were for entertaining and playacting the rustic life. The kitchen was fitted for opulent meals, which were to be served in a dining room decorated as a forest. Seats were imitation tree trunks, flower banks and trees lined the walls, branches covered the ceiling. The supposed grange was "a superb salon" of mirrored walls, coupled Corinthian pilasters, a painted ceiling and rose-taffeta drapes."[36]

The inspiration for this *folie* may have come from William Chambers' 1772 description of Miau Ting interiors: "The pavements of these rooms are sometimes laid out in parterres of flowers; amongst which are placed many rural seats, made of fine formed branches, varnished red to represent coral, but oftenest their bottom is full of a clear running water, which falls in rills from the sides of a rock in the center; many little islands float upon its surface, and move around as the current directs; some of them covered with tables for banquet; others with seats for the musicians; and others with arbors, containing beds of repose, with sofas, seats, and other furniture, for various uses."[37]

126

The *hameau*, neither farmstead or community, was a prototype for suburbia.

The *hameau* was a fitting stage set for a state of mind. It's picturesque pattern of detached rustic huts (with private amenities hidden) rambling through illusionary natural groves provided a public aura of independence and amiability. The curving roads with carefully placed clumps of trees masked any untenable realities that a straight *allée* might reveal. It was a *trompe-l'oeil* of a democratic landscape, an illusion of Arcadia ideal for its audience. It was universally consumed, and popular enough to be satirized by William Combe's (1812) Dr. Syntax: "I'll prose it here, I'll verse it there/And picturesque it everywhere."[38]

The picturesque landscape garden is almost universally justified as being natural, although its artificial elements are judiciously designed to amuse, to impress, to provoke, and to edify. Physical things convey spiritual messages through moralistic allegories; roads and rocks propagate political messages. Trees are sited *for the sake of* their symbolism, not *in order to* make ways and places for people. Depending on the viewer's proclivities, the patterns of each garden illustrates the degree of picturesque purity or the absence of picturesque taint. These episodes of artificial disorder are as contrived as their supposed antitheses, the geometric parterre and topiary. Nature is reordered according to "rules of the wild." The more perfect the illusion of reality, the more facile the deception. What is of interest is "the worked-upon, not the working, world."[39]

The worked-upon landscape separated itself from the working world. Like a *camera obscura*, or the painter's "Claude glass" (where views were reduced in size, their colors simplified to black and white), openings in hedges and in between groves framed selected diminished objects and distant working world views.

The picturesque view—on stage, on canvas, or on the landscape—depends on the vignette ("a centralized composition in a shallow space whose boundaries are undefined or shade off.")[40] The view of a plowed field (utilitarian, and therefore, not artistic) is separated from the giant vignette of green foliage in the foreground. The building (an object in the background, and therefore, dwarfed) is separated from the illusionary landscape of the imagination. In the picturesque garden small scale non-functioning reproductions of architecture devalue the original into an object, or series (since most picturesque gardens contain the same collection of *folies*), easily meaningful to the "absent-minded observer." As Tafuri notes: "The Gothic, Chinese, classical and eclectic pavilions inserted in the texture of a 'nature trained to be natural', are ambiguous objects. They allude to something other than themselves, losing their semantic autonomy. It is the same phenomenon that, a little later, will move into *major* architecture...."[41]

(81)

Paradoxically, movement through a formal grid of trees is free in any direction and the visitor sees where he is going, while along a picturesque path, movement and views are restricted to a series of prescribed scenarios.

THE HAMEAU AT CHANTILLY
Grand Environs de Paris

Château, gardens, and Museum of the Horse open everyday except Tuesday, 10:30–6:00. The interiors of the *hameau* are no longer exhibited.

1358	Chantilly, a fortress since the Middle Ages, pillaged. Pierre d'Orgement, owner.
1484	Guillaume de Montmorency, heir.
1552	Anne Montmorency, owner.
1524	Land transformed into large square agrarian garden.
1528–31	Pierre Chambiges reconstructs château, gallery and bath house.
1538	Jean Chocquet constructs terrace between park and château.
1560	Le Petit Château constructed; Jean Bullant, architect.
1567	Henri Montmorency, owner.
1643	Les Condé family, owners.
1662	André Le Nôtre, garden design, with Pierre and Claude Desgots, assistants. Jacques de Manse, hydraulic engineer. Daniel Gittard, architect.
1666	Grand parterre laid out.
1671–2	Grand Canal excavated. Hardouin-Mansart, architect.
1719	The Grand Stables begun, Jean Aubert, architect.
1756	Le Jeu de Paume built.
1772	The pavilion of Venus, the theater and the Château d'Enghien built.
1773	The *hameau* begun for the Prince de Condé. Julien David Leroy; English garden design.

THE BLACK LINE

127

Though architects and landscape designers may pursue different fantasies they have one thing in common. Both draw separate ideas before they are built or planted on the same site. To facilitate this endeavor a disastrous but convenient convention has been devised. Universities and offices allow a building, drawn by one person, or group, to receive a thick black line around it (probably with everything within the line eradicated) to be handed to another person, or group, to draw everything outside the black line. The black line is the buffer. Supposedly it is only seen on the piece of paper, but it seems to have made its mark on the built and planted landscape.

After the 1730s, traditional ways of organizing built and planted materials were scorned in favor of the new view of landscape as scenery, which became fashionable, and then correct, to be called natural. This view sailed across the Atlantic with the English and, in the righteous spirit of manifest destiny went West — to the ultimate misty escape — with those nineteenth century European trained landscape painters who equated the wilderness with freedom. They painted the American wilderness with even greater fervor than they would have their familiar English countryside.

The West (the illusionary Wild West) is where gardens were supposed to look especially natural. And natural was supposed to look as if God had personally dropped each seed onto the construction site. This was the God who smiled with infinite approval on the English landscape garden and seems to have not noticed the already existing town plans and plazas of New Spain and the beauty of the cultivated holdings. This God was eclectic and did not like rules. He was for the rights of Man and trees.

The English garden was random with a vengeance, subjective and designed to look natural; the West was wildly irregular, more untrimmed than the forests and Alps of Europe, a place for individuals; it really was rough and wild. Both England gardens and the wilderness were novelties. In both trees and men where free. Both were romanticized. They were the right image for modern man. It was nature that looked as if other men had never been there to push it around. Everyman's reward for successful revolt became a garden with a winding path and trees planted in wild array.

Concurrently, the symbolic and meaningful style for designing everyman's new buildings went in another direction. Architects were seduced by the machine, futurist dynamism, logical rationalism and functional science. They loved reinforced concrete, steel, glass, elevators, motors and speed, and the technological aesthetics of factories. A marriage was made: Happily, the social benefits of technological artifacts, homes and cities, could be enjoyed, while their industrial evils were avoided, if they were surrounded by picturesque-English-garden wildernesses.

This became the correct image of the modern landscape for the modern architecture of all the versions of the modern movement.

128

There were splendid prototypes to refer to. Many carefully made, random and manicured landscapes were excellent illusions of unspoiled even-better-than-raw-nature nature. It was possible for man to design a landscape to give the effect that it was a landscape not designed by man.

Modernism, for all its supposed basis in (among other things) Le Corbusier's "new kind of plan, both for the house and for the city ...(where)...the 'styles' are a lie"[42] fell into the eighteenth century habit of separating the work of the architect from the work of the landscape designer. Concerned with nature (if not precisely with landscape design), Le Corbusier separated nature into: the laws of nature according to which man (and the Parthenon) had been created, and romantic nature antithetical to the works of man. He placed his rational give-them-sun-light-and-air-so-they-won't-revolt housing in a picturesque-English-garden wilderness. Paths ramble through an undifferentiated and diverse scattering of trees. In drawings, vignettes of enormous trees frame the object buildings. Would-be styleless architecture was placed in a stylish scenery; architecture-in-itself was set in landscapes-for-fiction. While the white architecture of the brave new world was often a brilliant physical embodiment of modern intentions and fantasies, the landscapes (eventually parking lots instead of parks) were not.

If the site is not a piece of paper, the problems are different and more difficult. It is often impossible and inappropriate to return the land to a "former" condition that probably was never there. The problems are usually more prosaic and constricted: Cities need usable public parks and plazas, streets and the buildings along them need rows of trees to relate to each other. People need green shade to walk under and places to gather. Small gardens should appear grand and left-over sites need to look intended. Wiggly paths and a subjective scattering of "schrubish" are not the way to attain usability, clarity, and splendor.

Replacing the traditional objective methods of making inhabited landscapes with supposedly more free and creative solutions too often propagates confusion and expedient commercial formulae. Too much freedom to design has achieved a void in which it is difficult to design. Landscape architects persist in the idea that art is achieved by drawing their plans to emulate cubist, abstract expressionist, or minimalist painters, and more recently, "site conditioned-determined" (Robert Irwin's term) sculpture.

What looked like an ideal marriage didn't work out. When the modern movement in architecture married the picturesque-English-garden wilderness an unfortunate schism, in theory and practice, was initiated between the people who built buildings and the people who planted trees and planned the leftover spaces. The architects, absorbed by their object buildings, relinquished the job of landscape planning to the landscape designers. Though they talked of working together, their disparate views inhibited good intentions.

THE AGRARIAN VIEW

There was another way of making landscapes along with buildings before designers chose to forget it.

Traditionally Western agrarians cultivated the land in simple geometric patterns. Rectangular fields were cut from the wilderness or marked by roads and rows of trees on the plains. Orchards were planted in orderly grids. Crops grew between straight furrows. The logic of the land and concern for cultivation determined patterns on the land. This work used planted materials with the same utilitarian logic and pride in performance needed in the traditional use of building materials; the result often was a landscape of collected splendor.

These fields and farmsteads, simple and splendid, are everybody's inhabited homeland.

VILLA BARBARO
Maser

1560 Daniele and Marcantonio Barbaro, owners. Andrea Palladio, architect.

Privately owned. Open Tu/S/Sun 2–5

Villa Barbaro was made to be a working farm. Geometry on the land was a natural measure and mark of human existence and habitation. Habitable land was used to serve the orderly patterns of husbandry.

All inhabited places, rural and urban, are made by people: "...every region is distinguished from the wilderness in this respect: that it is an immense repository of labor...This land is thus not a work of nature; it is the work of our hands, our artificial homeland." Carlo Cattaneo[43]

"The charming landscape which I saw this morning is indubitably made up of some twenty or thirty farms. Miller owns this field, Locke that, and Manning the woodland beyond. But none of them owns the landscape. There is a property in the horizon which no man has but he whose eye can integrate all the parts, that is, the poet." R. W. Emerson[44]

THE AGRARIAN VIEW

129

In contrast to the Roman villa/pleasure gardens, used primarily for intermittent escape from the city, recreation, and meditation, the villas of the Veneto were agricultural estates managed by the discerning gentlemen who lived in them.

Lionello Puppi[45] compares the "unreal" recreational villas of Central Italy with the "real" (less spectacular, and therefore, less chronicled) villas of the Veneto.

The year-round presence of a new type of landlord, the city dweller, precluded using, in toto, architectural solutions from the preceding rural tradition. A suitable country retreat must fulfil new demands for comfort, recreation and splendor. Although the buildings (principally through the grandeur attained by Palladio) are influenced by the architecture of central Italy, the villa complex is not a "convenient place of *idle*, privileged refuge" but a working farm. In the villa of the Veneto there is "an active confrontation with nature, achieved in the structuring of this nature" and realized in the degree that "*structured* nature" (the garden) is integrated with the architecture. Complex functional needs "(utilitarian or spiritual, utilitarian and spiritual)" produced the villa. The "poetics" of the architecture, the garden, and the farm merge into a single ideology. The outdoor space functions as "intermediary" between the interior organization of the building and untamable nature. There is a constant exchange made more gradual by the garden plus the tamed fields and orchards. A further observation (clued by Tafuri) is that Palladio's objective method of planning allowed "*autobiographical*" display in interior wall decoration of the buildings, and an iconographic program in the immediate "secret garden" (as at the Villa Barbaro, Maser, entirely enclosed by the house and hillside). The public landscape is logically based on the history and economic events of the area, not on whim.

There is a dynamic relation between the *domus* and enlarged service structures of the farm operation, and the structured gardens, *oliveta* and *vineae*. The portico opens the building to the land on the ground floor; the second story loggia (not a device, but a functional response) provided communication between the men in the villa and the men on the land. The axis led straight to these fields and on to the next. *Allées* signaled roadways. Wind-rows identified

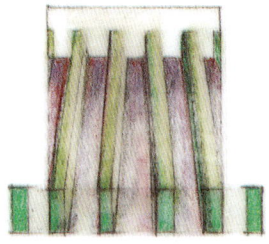

(90)

130

and on to the next. *Allées* signaled roadways. Wind-rows identified boundaries. The garden opened views to the land through balustrades and archways, along paths and hedges, from terraces and stairways, ahead and back again.

The individuality of the garden and the region (as splendid as any man has enjoyed) was found in the persistence of measure and rule, while the architecture (as noble as any nobleman required) was based on a similar, understood language. The magic of Venice worked with the functions of the farm. There was a merging of utility and ceremony, clarity and splendor, architecture and landscape.

The villas of the Veneto are farms that are gardens that are architecture. It is a landscape that is initially a useful means to cultivate the land and becomes an end that is desired for its beauty.

The agrarian garden emerged even in the midst of the modern movement. In 1925, despite his proclivity for floating towers over English parks, Le Corbusier said "Let us put the problem more logically."[46] In their housing project for Bordeaux, Le Corbusier and Pierre Jenneret designed an agrarian/sports garden. After examining garden city plans for new towns, Le Corbusier found the picturesque model too wasteful of space and too expensive and laborious to maintain. He designed a "honeycomb" plan of perimeter housing enclosing rectangular fields for farming and football, turnips and tennis. The vast expanses of English lawn were superseded by useful plots of cultivation bordered by fruit orchards. The project was planned on a grid of straight tree-lined streets.

"A farmer acts as superintendent and manager of a grouping. The agricultural labourer is deserting the countryside; with three shifts of eight hours each in operation, the artisan here becomes his own agricultural labourer and produces an important part of the food he consumes. Architecture? Town planning? The logical study of the cell and its functions in relation to the mass may furnish a solution rich in results."[47] The Le Corbusier who wrote "Geometry is the language of man"[48] proposed an agrarian landscape.

The traditional pattern of the agricultural community and modernist social purpose merged.

| THE STEAD: farmstead, homestead, a traditional farm. | An early Gothic definition of *land* was plowfield. | The English *champion* (from champagne) meant a countryside of fields. | A *landschaft* was a cluster of buildings surrounded by fields, then forest. | "A landscape is the antithesis of the wilderness." Stilgoe |

"Steads varied in form across central and Western Europe, but the essential pattern, a rough rectangle or square made of buildings and fences, extended from the Danube to the British Isles. ... Having a stead, a house and yard, meant having some fragment of outdoor space secured from chaos and made profitable.... Holding a house and yard and fulfilling its responsibilities of the *landschaft* enabled a family to hold its spatial and social position indefinitely."[49]

The traditional stead consists of a permanent home together with a stable, barn, and granary or dovecote all connected to form a wall around a yard or court.

Though the *landscaft* was small "its wholeness gave it strength."

"As the city grows, patrician estates often are turned over to several families of tenants. In the case of large courtyard houses, such as the Roman *domi*, exterior access to the generously-sized rooms permits each room to become a house in itself, a private apartment. This is what Caniggia has called *tabernizzazione* of the *domus*, or the transformation of the *domus* into an urban apartment house."[50]

(The outside facade of a quadrangular complex is called its perimeter; the inside facade, facing the yard, or court, or plaza, is not public, and therefore, there is no name for it.)

Rather than the *hameau*, we can pattern our towns on the stead.

The stead can be seen as prototype of the perimeter block.

There are traditional ways of using plant material as architecture with agrarian logic and visual splendor:

131 An enclosed field of grass,

132 or a meadow of poppies.

133 A wheat field in front of a farmhouse,

134 water leading to the horizon,

135 or two oaks framing the road.

136 Two cypresses announcing a villa,

137 a row of trees around a soccer field.

138 A grid of trees to walk through in any direction.

139 A line of trees reflected in the water,

140 or enclosing a field of chard.

141 A green rectangle drawn on the ground becomes a green triangle to the eye.

142 Lines on paper become a path,

143 or a building,

144 a passage,

145 or a tree.

146	147	148	149	150

Two lines of trees are a road,	or the shape of the sky in the country.	Buildings bounding a street cut out a piece of sky in a city.	A path in a park is an entrance.	An arch of light is a gateway to drive through.

And in the West, similar, simple solutions:

151
A boundary of eucalyptus,

152
three trees against the sky,

153
an almond orchard,

154
and street trees in a town.

155
Or palms.

Twin palms,

or a processional *allée*, proudly announcing the entrance to a home.

The grid of vineyards relentlessly carpeting the valleys.

Rows of purple plums in the country.

A green in the center of a city.

IV
GREEN ARCHITECTURE

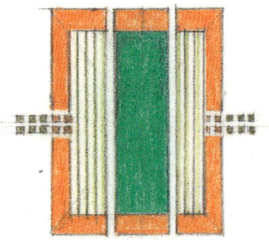

**The Formal/Agrarian View
(105)**

**Green Architecture
(111)**

**The Egalitarian Grid
(118)**

**Grids
on
the Port of St. Francis
(123)**

THE FORMAL/AGRARIAN VIEW

There is a formal/agrarian view of making landscapes that is utilitarian and beautiful.

This view proudly admits that landscapes, like buildings, are made by men.

In the formal/agrarian view the inhabited landscape, and the habitable city, are the result of the collective imagination. Though each private *primary element* is made and cared for by individuals, the whole landscape, urban or rural, is in the public view.

There is a familiar resemblance between the patterns of cultivation and urban plans. Formal and agrarian views are based on similar comprehensive patterns. Furrows deepen into streets, trees become columns, and cleared fields become plazas. Grids of orchards become the ground plans of buildings. Buildings are planned in conjunction with streets. Green walls reinforce inhabited corridors. Farmsteads are perimeter blocks. Until political romantics sought to free the trees along with the people, this habit of planned order (rather than planned disorder) was a model for avenues and *allées*, palaces and farms, parks and gardens.

VILLA GIULIA
Rome

1519 Cardinal Antonio del Monte, original owner.
1533 Cardinal Giovanni Maria del Monte, owner.
1539 Jacopo Mellghino, garden architect.
1550 Giovanni, now Pope Julius III.
1551 Giorgio Vasari, architect. Michelangelo, architect. Bartolomeo Ammannati, architect. Giacomo da Vignola, architect.

Open daily except Monday.

Renaissance villas began as *vigne* (farms and vineyards). In spring and fall Roman laborers fled their tenements and nobles left their palaces to celebrate the satisfaction of the harvest and the joys of the vintage. The workers and the owners — all of whom were concerned — gathered together to reap the rewards of their mutual endeavors.[51]

Villa Giulia, for all its splendor, began as a *vigna*.

The Legend of Villa Giulia:

At Villa Giulia
1.
The *facade* fronts the *mountain*. The *axis* follows the line of the valley. *Furrows* and *walls* from the vigna widen to become *buildings*.
2.
The *view* from the *vestibule* of the *casino* extends through *doorways* to the farthest *garden*. The *portico* is a half-circle; *proscenium wings* for the *courtyard-theater*. The flat site needs levels. *Stairways* curve down to a *nymphaeum* and on to a *pool* in its island. Here *caryatids* support double *loggia* on their heads. Below is the dank *grotto*.
3.
The *walls* of the theater are *doors* to the fields. Toward the theater *bays* and *niches* house gods. Toward the *mountains* walls house farm tools.

(106)

There is a correlation between the love of the garden with the *schism* between architecture and the landscape:

"...the pleasant flatland is never a plough field, nor a rich lotus meadow good for pasture, but *garden* ground covered with flowers...with a castle in the middle of it. The aspens are delighted in, not because they are good for 'coach-making men' to make cart-wheels of, but because they are shady and graceful;... And the ideal occupation of mankind is not to cultivate either the garden or the meadow, but to gather roses..."[52]

When men loved their private garden they devised a way to make an artificial construct of an untouched nature. The illusionary images and moral implications of this picturesque scenery were myopically extended from the private garden to the public landscape. Each man's castle was detached from his neighbor's and made a make-believe ornament wrapped in illusion. The historic urban fabric was intended to be replaced by picture book scenery scattered with occasional monuments and relics. "The 'Voisin' scheme...safeguards the relics of the past and enshrines them harmoniously in a framework of trees and woods. For material things too must die, and these green parks with their relics are in some sort cemeteries, carefully tended, in which people may breathe, dream and learn. In this way the past becomes no longer dangerous to life, but finds instead its true place within it."[53]

Where once a garden was an untended meadow in a grove, it has come to resemble a carefully-tended-to-look-untended stage set. It could no longer pretend innocence.

The landscape designer's fantasy was fulfilled in his landscape of the imagination; the architect's attention was riveted on his object building. This separation of the intuitive planting from the rational building was a picturesque view that invaded the twentieth century.

When history and the straight line were erased from the natural landscape, it was hoped that man-made injustices would disappear from the scene. What did disappear was the public realm of streets and plazas comprehended and enjoyed by the people.

Architecture books show plans of buildings isolated on the white page; landscape books illustrate the gardens and cut the house plan from the picture.

There is a correlation between the love of the farm and the *integration* of landscape and architecture:

"...now it is time for me to dig the sweet soil..."
Columella.

When men loved their agrarian holdings they sited their buildings to view the fields. They delighted in the spectacle of the crops and the ceremony of the harvests. Urban men commissioned formal/agrarian buildings to glorify rural gardens.

As the architecture came to glorify the men themselves, and their autocratic institutions rather than the rural fields and the urban plazas, architecture took on another meaning.

There is a correlation between the love of the city and the *integration* of landscape and architecture:

"...precisely because the city [and the countryside] is preeminently a collective fact it is defined by and exists in those works that are of an essentially collective nature. Although such works arise as a means of constituting the city, they soon become an end, and this is their being and their beauty. The beauty resides both in the laws of architecture [and cultivation] which they embody and in the collective's reasons for desiring them."[54]

"...the men who could run to the piazza in time to take part in the municipal election, a party demonstration, or a street fight"[55] controlled the political life in 1920 Italy.

"St. Mark's Square in Venice, where the large piazza forms a meaningful transition between the dense labyrinth of the city and the glittering expanse of the sea..."[56] is a particularly splendid collective artifact in that "preeminently collective fact" — the city.

Lesser public artifacts are as beloved by the people to whom they belong. Utility combines with ceremony; logic with illusion; architecture is landscape.

In the 1970's, some architects and planners began to see the unhappy results of modern architecture/picturesque landscape marriage. They looked back to traditional ways of planning towns and cities. Many landscape architects, strangled by their serpentine paths, felt lost in the wilderness they had been taught to prefer.

GREEN ARCHITECTURE
is
where landscape and architecture overlap:

Furrowed fields and orchards; arbors, *mails* and *allées*;
walls with doors and windows;
promenades;
in and outdoor theaters of green, water, marble or plush;
balustrades and public stairways and ramps;
gates, gatehouses, gates in walls, gateways over streets;
portals, thresholds and foyers;
porticoes;
squares and greens: common, bowling and civic;
pools for swimming and reflection; pool houses and cabañas;
courts: fore, rear, ceremonial or tennis;
balconies and belvederes; grandstands and circus tents;
fairs, expositions, resorts and amusement parks;
greenhouses and rooms for the wind;
parks and park buildings;
canopies and awnings;
pergolas;
outdoor cafés, sidewalks with signs, lights and trees;
passages, paths, enclosed streets and fences;
lobbies and galleries for waiting, shopping, strolling;
aediculae;
entrances: the front stoop; porches (front and back);
the backyard and the middle block;
housebridges and bridgehouses;
wings and platforms for performing, waiting and diving;
canals, grottoes, *rochers; bosquets* and their green rooms;
public boathouses and houseboats;
gazebos, pavilions, pagodas and temples;
topi- and avi-aries;
railway, snow, garden and backyard sheds; barns and coops;
landings; covered bridges, barges and piers;
stadiums, bandstands and picnic tables;
coves and alcoves;
colonnades;
and
the vestibule, veranda, dog trot, roof garden, deck, loggia,
balcony, piazza, trellis, terrace, atrium, patio, peristyle,
exedra, sunroom, *ramblas*, courtyard, cloister, recreational
center, pool house, public bath, baseball diamond, parcourse,
running track, campsite, recreational vehicle hook-up, stoa,
villa and château with its garden,
grids of street trees,
and the views from all these places
to
the next.

GREEN ARCHITECTURE
is
the common ground between architecture and landscape
and
the familiar resemblance between formal and agrarian gardens.

Common ground (customary, and therefore, often invisible) is somewhere between closed privacy and open exposure. It is where the forms of the hills shape the forms of the buildings. On common ground there is an ambiguity between public and private, real and fantastic, outdoors and indoors, nature and technology, and most other things.

People move through trees and thresholds as easily as they see the two in the same glance. There is no line where landscape stops and architecture begins. The park leads to the building; the building makes a view of the park. Paths clarify rather than obscure.

A rectangle of green on the ground rises at right angles to become the green wall of a building. A field of grass cut from the forest is a green theater. The green rectangle becomes a triangle to the eye. Permanent and impermanent elements merge in plan and as elevations of buildings, nonbuildings, buildings that are not quite buildings and trees that are almost buildings.

When
"as in corridors of a house, where the human step circulates as if it skirted the angles of furniture and shoes never wear out, the place has the character of an immense collective apartment...."
where
"palaces and churches...play the part of great divans of repose, table of entertainment, expanses of decoration. And somehow the splendid common domicile, familiar, domestic and resonant, also resembles a theater...."
Henry James
The Aspern Papers, 1888

Green architecture is not just green. Henry James is writing about Venice. Venice is pink and grey (unless one counts the green corridors of water and sky). Venice is, however, where landscape and architecture overlap. The "splendid common domicile" is made of connecting walls with doors and windows enclosing especially uncommon paths of movement. Venice is a collective undertaking. Built walls grow from the canals they shape. The division between nature and art is invisible.

The colonnade is a more common collective element that is built and planted, architecture and landscape, formal and agrarian, appropriate to everyday use and special ceremony.

The colonnade is a green *allée* of trees shading a rural path or a white row of columns announcing the entrance to an urban building. It is for people to walk under, to see out of, or to view from a distance. Fronting a court house, it is a civic element; in front of a church, it is sacred ground. In Constantinople or Bologna it is a commercial street; at St. Peter's in Rome it is a sacred way. It is Mayan at Chichen Itzá, Hellenistic on the Palatine Hill, medieval in a monastery, classical in a sanctuary, neo-classical in a French library, and rational in Terrangi's Casa del Popolo. In France, Mansart was inspired by Colonna for his colonnade of ideas at Versailles; in California the mission architects were following Spanish/Mexican tradition and functional necessity. Recalling Rome or the monarchy, the colonnade is "a superbly controlled design, like the policies of Colbert or an argument of Descartes."[57] Remembering rural *allées*, it is Viel de Saint-Maux's monumental architecture symbolizing agriculture.[58]

"When people come to inspect ...farmsteads, it is not to see collections of pictures... but collections of fruit." Varro, ca. 120 BC

While we in the United States have venerated the agricultural garden and enshrined the American farmstead as part of our heritage, we have systematically erased the agrarian elements of landscapes from our ideas of beauty in the garden. The plowed field, wind-rows and *allées* admired by travelers as beautiful entrances to Palladian villas and French estates have been ignored, or derided, by garden theorists. We have gone along with the view that the landscape should be arcadian scenery.

The simple is not seen as the splendid.

Flower fields and orchards have been ostracized as practical and therefore not poetic. "Food," writes agricultural historian Robert West, "was grown by peasants and farmers, not by ladies and gentlemen. The British homeowner who enjoyed gardening and its harvest secluded the operation at the rear of his residence. Americans copied their *statis fix*."

"The English appraised the New World too meanly. It was to them a carcass from which to tear pieces for their belly's sake, a colony, a place to despise a little. They gave to it parsimoniously, in a slender Puritan fashion. But the Spaniard gave magnificently, with a generous sweep, wherever he was able."[59]

When California was New Spain, there were certain visual statements on the land. These "patterns of settlement,"[60] devised by farmers and ranchers, were ignored by designers looking to English texts and New England models for ways to make the West look civilized. Agri-culture was not anglo-culture. They wanted the landscape to look like scenery. They cut down the orchards and planted pastorals.

Later potential agrarian gardens were bulldozed by suburban-renewal. Acres of rich California flower farms and orchards were destroyed in order to scatter and isolate ranchhouses in small berms of lawn and plastic wildernesses.

Rather than designing more decorated scenarios, these less than happy no-places might become collective landscapes. Fields of artichokes, marigolds and purple plums could unite the homes and the inhabitants with useful and beautiful patterns of settlement.

A canny appraisal of the present has lead many enterprising Californians to return to live on, and from, the land. The products of their farms are in demand in the cities. Former urbanites have created specialty farms to supply city markets and restaurants dependent on fresh (and fancy) fruits and vegetables for the new California cuisine. They are their own bosses, and for them, the farm is again a paradise garden. Proud of their work, and cognizant of agricultural aesthetics, they have made agrarian gardens.

A greenhouse dwelling, fields of Spanish lavender, a meadow of California poppies, two boathouses, a wisteria arbor, a wall of Monterey cypress and vines, and palms to celebrate the entrance, make an agrarian landscape on a slough where the Petaluma River divides Marin from Sonoma County as it enters San Francisco Bay.

THE EGALITARIAN GRID

 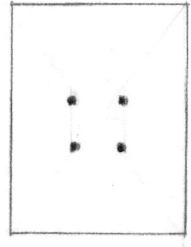 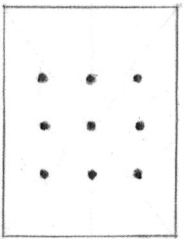 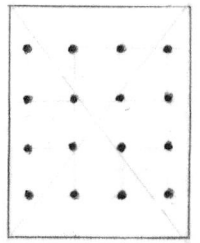 

"initial point"　　square field　　central point　　central field　　central crosspoint

When straight lines were banned from picturesque scenery, traditional streets were abandoned on the drawing board. The public world was neglected in favor of islands of private living along meandering bucolic paths. But this happened only later in the United States. Initially, practical men preferred tradition. The collective grid of tree lined streets connecting private houses to public squares was the American urban and agrarian ideal.

Historically during periods of colonialization, the grid ("One of the great inventions of the human mind."[61]) was the symbol of orderly urban life. The Egyptian character for a land district is the grid; the Chinese character is a "nine-field"; Greek colonies, Roman castrum, and medieval bastides used rectangular grid patterns for urban and rural development.

The practical divided square is the secular equivalent and archetype of the sacred magic circle with its central point. The grid is understandable, economical and egalitarian. Straight streets intersecting at right-angles to form rectangular blocks symbolize emancipation from previous inequalities and relatively fair intentions:[62] The perfect symbol for the young United States.

Ancient and medieval city centers had time to grow organically. In New Spain, New England and colonial and frontier towns, things happened faster, — and on *Virgin Land*.[63]

The first town in the United States, St. Augustine, Florida, was a grid centered on a square plaza. Examples abound.[64] The settlements of New Spain (which in 1790 extended from the Pacific to Florida and the Mississippi) were planned according to the Spanish *Laws of the Indies* (1573). This "Royal Ordinance for the Laying Out of New Cities, Towns or Villages" specified a rectangular central plaza enclosed by a grid of streets crossing at right angles. Custom is practical.

In 1681 William Penn introduced the urban grid to New England at Philadelphia. Originally, Penn planned to have people live close to the town square and travel straight wide streets to their rectangular fields, but the town and the demand for land grew. Innovation was necessary; the urban grid was extended over the wilderness. Rectangular "liberty land" farms were surveyed. The grid of enlightened optimism, drawn on a piece of paper, preceded the settlement of the land. People realized that some municipal control over land development was compatible with a democratic society.[65]

Street grids and the agrarian sectioning of the wilderness were separate, but similar. Their histories interweave. Together they structured the myth of democracy.

Thomas Jefferson's agrarian philosophy rested on European cultural ideas: Virgil's poetic praise of husbandry; the Physiocrats' philosophical acclaim of agriculture as the primary source of each man's wealth; Abbé Raynal's political image of the farmer as a republican symbol rather than the humble and contented peasant in the pastoral scenery. The *Virgin Land* provided unprecedented possibilities for their political implications and implementation. In Virginia, Jefferson proposed that every landless adult be given a homestead from the public domain. To provide more land for more people, he mapped out fourteen new states (named Sylvania, Metropolamia, and Polypotamia, etc.).

Jefferson proposed dividing the Western Territory into squares of 100 geographical miles with straight lines running north-south and east-west every ten miles. With Jefferson's "hundreds," the non-varying grid and the square subdivision became basic American land measurements.

The Roman *centuria* consisted of 100 square *heredia*. At its center a north-south axis intersected with an east-west crossaxis. The religious symbolism of the center was twofold: The square (*quadra*) implied a static form of equilibrium while the quarter (*quartarius*) had a dynamic cosmological meaning. The old word for crosspoint was *umbilicus* (navel) or center of the world.[66] Research has not proved that Jefferson knew of the Roman centuriation but his "perfect scheme for ordering a wilderness *tabula rasa*"[67] gave the American farmstead the same north-south, east-west grid pattern seen on the plains of the Po Valley.

Jefferson's enlightened abstraction was not adopted, but on May 20, 1785, Congress authorized a survey of the Western Territories into six-mile by six-mile townships. The mile square grid followed.

Section lines north-south, east-west, like lines drawn on a piece of white paper, were drawn on two-thirds of the present United States. The abstract and egalitarian grid predated roads and fields, fences and structures. Each square (however unequal topographically) was ideally democratic. On the spot "section corrections" would placate individual men and contours. The grid on the piece of paper/wilderness determined the future views of and from the American landscape.

By 1820 the abstract grid was a permanent image on the national imagination. Settlers and adventurers understood its arbitrary/democratic logic. Tradition and geometry were law; drawings predated data; maps were mandatory. A farmer who wanted a piece of land located and announced its section number on the map, paid his money and proceeded to plant his paradise.

"With each surge of westward movement [writes Henry Nash Smith] a new community came into being. These communities devoted themselves not to marching onward but to cultivating the earth. They plowed the virgin land and put in crops, and the great Interior Valley was transformed into a garden: for the imagination, the Garden of the World...a collective representation, a poetic idea ...that defined the promise of American life."[68]

When the garden was no longer a paradise, "the myth of the garden" survived in the collective imagination and in the physical patterns of the landscape it had made. Straight roads following the section lines extended into the horizon. The mile square township roads separate fields. Row crops follow the grid. Farms houses are oriented "Square to the Road, Hogs to the East."[69] The farmer in the Midwest, much later the fruit grower in California, settled the wilderness and shaped agrarian landscapes according to the urban grid of Philadelphia. "Phrases such as 'a square deal' and 'he's a four-square man' entered the national vocabulary as expressions of righteousness and fairness. By the 1860's the grid objectified national, not regional, order, and no one wondered at rural space marked by urban rectilinearity."[70]

The imagination of that 1785 Congress was captured by the visual, as well as the political, implications of drawing lines of latitude and longitude on pieces of paper and parcels of land. Congressmen repeatedly delivered speeches comparing their land-planning to painting.[71]

Today the Department of Agriculture, as a means of preventing sheet and rill erosion of the topsoil by wind and water, prescribes compulsory terracing, strip cropping, crop rotation, and contour plowing. The end is site-conditioned-determined sculpture appreciated by transcontinental passengers and the farmers (who have contests of land art as well as land yields). The eighteenth century Congress (to a degree they could not have anticipated) and the twentieth century Soil Conservation Service (to a degree they are totally aware of) have achieved a collective agrarian landscape of extraordinary beauty during the day; at night grids of lights blaze billboards of intended egalitarianism.

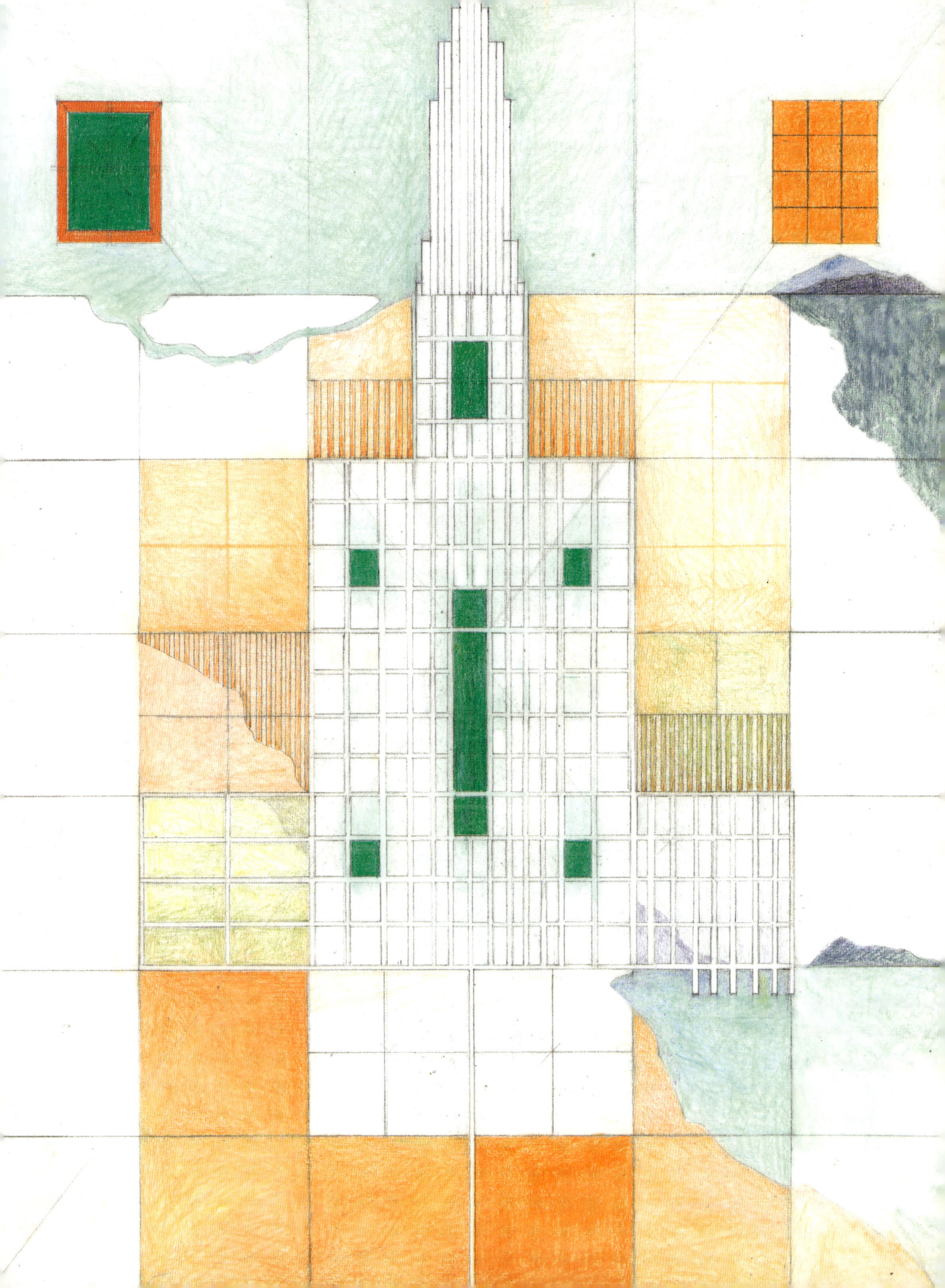

GRID ON THE FOOT OF ST. FRANCIS

**GRIDS
ON THE PORT OF
ST. FRANCIS**

San Francisco is a gridded city. As it grew, the grid accommodated. Streets were drawn straight from the harbor, uninflected over hills, to the Pacific in the west; and straight from North Beach, over hills, to the San Bruno Mountains to the south.

San Francisco is a comprehensible collective landscape. There is order in its gridded plan, which connects each building with its neighbor and to the farthest point on the grid; there is enclosure in the peninsular surrounded by water and a mountain range, and in each corridor of street enclosed by a common domicile of inhabited walls (often more decorated on the outside than inside); there is magic in the urban furrows, which end in hilltop parks, civic plazas, and green rectangles in the harbor and at the Pacific.

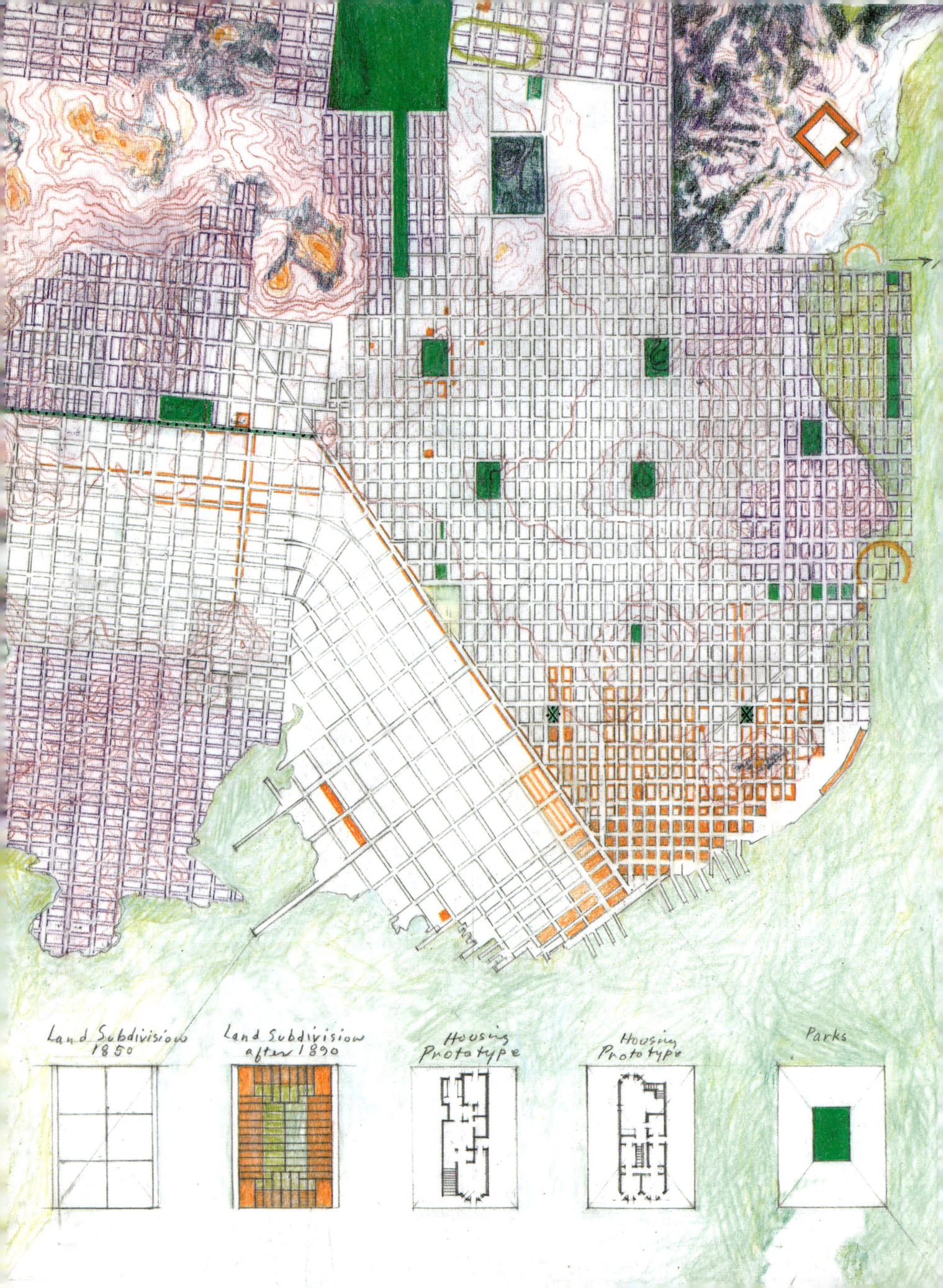

SAN FRANCISCO
California

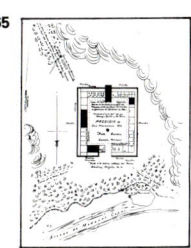

165

Jean-Jacques Voiget, a Swiss who had lived in Chile, used the gridiron pattern traditional for laying out colonialized Spanish-American ideal cities. When O'Farrell suggested using a street layout, adapted to the topography, he was dissuaded by landowners. The grid accommodated their speculative activities and San Francisco's explosive growth.[72]

The grid symbolized urbanism.

The 25 foot grid was based on the juxtaposition of living room and stairway, or two bedrooms, or bath, kitchen and corridor.

The grid accommodates the interaction of public city structure and private house plan.

1776 Spanish establish *presidio* and Mission of San Francisco de Asis.
1834 Military *presidio* converted into civic *pueblo*.
1835 City center shifted from *pueblo* to port.
1839 Original grid around cove plotted by Jean-Jacques Voiget.
1846 California becomes American Territory.
1851 California becomes a state.
1847 Population of San Francisco: 860. Jasper O'Farrell extends grid west and south.
1848 The Gold Rush.
1851 William Eddy extends the grid.
1854 Population of San Francisco: 50,000.

The *presidio* was a military settlement of barracks, stores, shops, stables, and dwellings. It was a quadrangular complex around a square plaza. The *pueblo* extended from the center of the *presidio* plaza for twenty-seven miles.

166

To many people the West is a phantom place always somewhere ahead on the road. To a native San Franciscan the West is someplace within sight of the Pacific (or, at least, of the Bay.)

(125)

The Marina District was built on land filled for the Panama Pacific International Exposition. When the fair's Tower of Lights went out in 1915, the Yacht Harbor and Bernard Maybeck's Palace of Fine Arts remained.

The Marina is enclosed by the Marina Green and the Bay to the north, the Palace of Fine Arts and the *presidio* (its naturally barren hills now covered by grids of eucalyptus forest) to the west, the Pacific Heights to the south, and a grassy knoll planted with eucalyptus, Monterey cypress, and some ceremonial palms to the east.

The filled land is flat but its streets furrow over the hills to the valley of Market Street.

Each perimeter block of the Marina, Pacific Heights, and most of the gridded city enclose a green rectangle of back yards. Without setback, the front facades of the houses form the street; the three or four story rear walls enclose the interior gardens. Each garden is private and fenced; these might have been private/public formal, picturesque, and agrarian gardens with axes from the Palace of Fine Arts to Fort Mason, and from the Marina Green to Chestnut Street.

Hilltops became parks. Initially too difficult for construction, they remained fields of herbs and grasses; later they were planted in formal or picturesque patterns within their rectangular edge.

In San Francisco every street ends in the Bay, or the Pacific, or both. To drive down some streets is to descend, quickly, into a congested urban street or plaza; to drive up is to head straight into the sky.

From these straight streets everyone gets a clear view of where they are, where they are going and where they have been. Street trees and mid-block gardens terrace to the Bay, providing dark green to the white city.

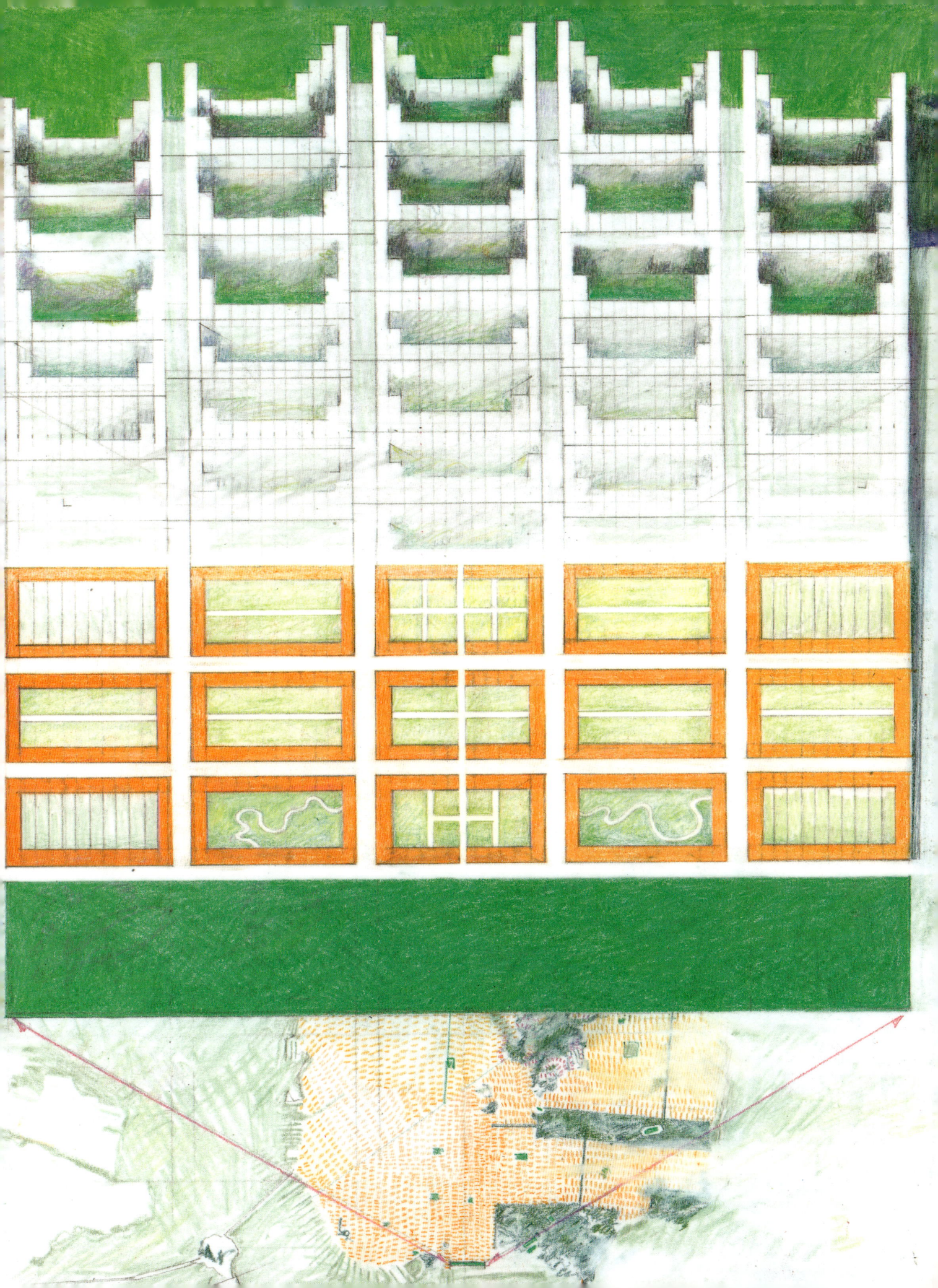

"The city," writes David Wyatt, "that rises like an exhalation, San Francisco, burns and rises again and again."[73] Wyatt likens "this panorama of 'dissolving views' " to the constant Californian condition of 'sudden wonder' induced by a landscape where the "survivors [are] the stunned occupants of a perpetual present."[74]

The California wilderness has been discovered and deified; simultaneously, the California landscape has been developed and destroyed. Still, whatever Californians perpetrate on their idolized land, they justify it by a desire to service the California dream (individual and collective) of an even more comfortable representation of paradise.

In the West people grid the ground as a way of grounding a culture. Space is changed into place and places change as fast as time.

In 1905 Henry James found California "a sort of prepared but unconscious and inexperienced Italy, the primitive *plate*, in perfect condition, but with the impression of History all yet to be made."[75] Feeling free of history, living in the present in a landscape that easily provided basic needs, Californians indulged in fantasy. There are two kinds of fantasy: escape and planning. Both have shaped fiascos. Nature is no sooner discovered as paradise, and cultivated as a garden, than human nature sees it as a landscape of golden opportunities. Valleys are flooded and agrarian gardens paved over in the service of public plans and private whim or profit. Today, more experienced Californians can consciously attempt to reshape some of these fiascos back to their cultivated (if not original) splendor.

In cities we are obsessed with nature and with paradise. Nature as paradise is the recreational garden. We use it to improve our bodies, and incidentally, our minds and our chances for immortality. Since few people today can afford a private paradise, the public landscape can provide some of that paradise lost.

In cities we can decide that a selected rectangle in a grid will be green. This piece of hallowed ground becomes particular, possessed...a garden. A square of grass is a garden. A tree is a garden. We plot a path, enclose a lawn, order trees, and make the water rise. We make an urban park into everybody's paradise.

The Marina Green is an urban paradise. It is flat, open, a green rectangle of grass surrounded on three sides by water. It is an edge of the city that is a center of the world for those people who rush there, down straight streets, each morning and evening, to run or bike or throw a ball, or to sit and stare at the view and the water.

There is magic in the collective image of San Francisco. The collision of the formal grid and the natural topography produced occasions for civic architecture, for green rectangles ascending hilltops and extending onto the water.

There is magic in the collective image of California as paradise; it is a paradise of found public landscape (rather than a paradise within). For when Western man ended his trek westward, to George Eliot's "golden fruit upon a tree/All out of reach," he was rewarded with an Edenic landscape that seemed a beginning. Experiencing the landscape became a substitute for thinking about ideas. Poets had love affairs with the land; pathetic fallacies were plentiful. But paradise was lost, or changed, as fast as it was found.

Landscapes with buildings are where history takes place. The found wilderness may initially dictate human behavior and, to the degree people respond to it, thought; but people are not statues or animals set in the scenery. They shape the landscape of facts to the landscape of their imagination when they inhabit it. There is nowhere else to go.

In 1923 Le Corbusier spoke out against "Eyes which do not see."[76] He wanted people to see the beauty of "day to day" constructions "there under our eyes" — things which "respond to a need."[77]

In California we need to be free enough of eighteenth and nineteenth century bias to see and recover the logical and rewarding ways of using trees and herbs, crops and flowers in conjunction with buildings that made our former Edenic agrarian gardens and towns.

"Someday we will have to plow up the malls to plant something we can eat" said Arnold "Jete" Rota, a central Valley *vaguero* in 1986.

Now that the noble homeowner is cultivating his own garden the furrows can come up to the front door and through it. The clarity and beauty of these agrarian elements in our private gardens would connect the private garden with the public town and reshape the landscape to an earlier collective image.

The agrarian garden is as paradisical as the much touted picturesque and formal gardens.

The three views of, and from, the formal, picturesque and agrarian garden reveal their common sources and eventual dissimilarities.

Moulin-Joli and Ermenonville were cultivated holdings decorated with some art and architecture. They were working farm gardens; a paradise that was part of the agricultural economy. These early picturesque gardens were propagated by the same georgic literature that inspired the American ideal of the agrarian garden in the West. People's fantasies were different.

Originally, Villa Barbero, less so Villa Giulia, were as appreciated for their harvests and vineyards as for their architecture, green theaters and grottos. Their orderly planted and built patterns on the land were glorified into formal gardens. The connections of the land with the buildings remained similar in plan; the elevations of the buildings were more variegated. People's views, of themselves and others, changed.

Agrarian gardens were precursors of formal gardens and urban settlements. They are our earliest and most consistent ways of shaping the inhabited landscape: "our splendid common domicile." The habit of clearing rectangular fields in forests continued in the public squares of cities. Farmsteads became perimeter complexes of dwellings. Fields marked by rows of trees became civic plazas in their colonnades. Furrows widen into corridor streets, orchard grids become ground plans for temples, towns and territories. Green rectangles remain symbols of paradise. People change; their views change; their views of the landscape change; their imaginations of paradise gardens change. Prejudices are punctured; contradictions can be enjoyed.

NOTES:

1 George Seferis, "On Stage" from "Three Poems" quoted by S. S. Draenos in "Thinking Without a Ground," *Hannah Arendt: Recovery of the Public World* (St. Martin's Press, New York, 1979), p.223.
2 Arthur O. Lovejoy, *The Great Chain of Being* (Harvard University Press, 1936), p.16.
3 Christopher Hussey, *The Picturesque* (London, 1927), p. 128.
4 Stephen Switzer, *Ichnographia Rustica* (London, 1718), I, p.55, 317 & 273 quoted by John Dixon Hunt, *Gardens and Groves* (London, 1986), p.187.
5 Christopher Hussey, *English Gardens and Landscapes 1700–1750* (London, 1967), p.123.
6 Tom Turner, *English Garden Design* (London, 1986), p.86.
7 On Rousham see Paula Dietz, *The Painted Garden* (Vanity Fair, April, 1986), pp.85–91, and J. D. Hunt, op.cit., pp.211–216.
8 See Dora Wiebenson, *The Picturesque Garden in France* (Princeton University Press, 1978), pp.87–88.
9 Monique Mosser and Geoffrey James, *Morbid Symptoms* (Princeton Architectural Press, 1986), p.50.
10 G. Cuppini & A.M. Matteucci, *Ville del Bolognese* (Zanichelli, Bologna, 1969), pp. 360–1.
11 See Eugenio Battisti, "Natura Artificiosa to Natura Artificialis," *The Italian Garden* (Dumbarton Oaks, 1972), p.12.
12 Ibid., pp.10–12.
13 Pliny *Epistles, V, 6*, quoted by E. MacDougall in "Ars Hortulorum: Sixteenth Century Garden Iconography," *The Italian Garden* (Dumbarton Oaks, 1972), p.47.
14 Shakespeare, *As You Like It*, quoted by Hunt, op.cit., p.43, in reference to gardens.
15 E. Battisti, op.cit., p.30.
16 M. Mosser, op.cit., p.51.
17 Homer, *The Odyssey* (Bantam, New York, 1962), p.99.
18 Sir Henry Wotton, *Elements of Architecture*, 1624, quoted in J. D. Hunt, op.cit., p.10.
19 Vitruvius, *de Architettura*, V.vi,9, quoted in Alberti, *The Ten Books on Architecture*, quoted by S. Land, "Genesis of the Landscape Garden," *The Picturesque Garden* (Dumbarton Oaks, 1974), p.18.
20 Horace Walpole, *World I*, No.6, p.37, quoted in D. Wiebenson, op.cit., p.60.
21 Manfredo Tafuri, *Theories and History of Architecture* (Harper and Row, New York, 1980), p.82.
22 M. Le Bris, *Le Paradis Perdu* (Paris, 1981), quoted in M. Mosser, op.cit., p.50.
23 J. D. Hunt, op.cit., pp.191–2.
24 Ibid., p. 196.
25 Joseph Spence, *Observations, Anecdotes and Characters of Books and Men* (Oxford, 1966), quoted in J. D. Hunt, op.cit., p.196.
26 T. Whately, *Observations on Modern Gardening* (London, 1770), quoted in D. Wiebenson, op.cit., p.32.
27 G.L. Ferri de San-Constante, *Londres et les Anglois*, III, p.189, quoted in D. Wiebenson, op.cit., p.38.
28 William Shenstone, quoted in Christopher Thacker *The History of Gardens* (University of California Press, 1979), pp.201–1.
29 T. Whately, *Observations*, p. 162, quoted in D. Wiebenson, op.cit., p.48.
30 W. Mason, *The English Garden* (1778), p.33: "Mr. Southcote was the introducer, or rather the inventor of the *ferme ornée*, for it may be presumed that nothing more than the term is of French extraction." quoted in D. Wiebenson, op. cit., .98. See D. Wiebenson for study of the *ferme ornée*.
31 Ibid., p.99.
32 Claude-Henri Watelet, *Essai sur les jardins* (Paris, 1764), quoted in William Howard Adams *The French Garden 1500–1800* (George Braziller, New York, 1979), p.116.
33 See D. Wiebenson for study of Moulin-Joli.
34 J. De Lille, *Les Jardins*, pp.71–72, quoted in D. Wiebenson, op.cit., p.18.
35 Ibid., p.99.
36 Ibid., p.100.
37 William Chambers, *Dissertation on Oriental Gardening* (1772), quoted in D. Wiebenson, op.cit., p.58.
38 William Combe, *The Tour of Dr. Syntax* (1812), quoted in Ann Bermingham, *Landscape and Ideology* (University of California Press, 1986), p.83.
39 Barbara Maria Stafford, *Voyage Into Substance* (MIT, 1984), p. 4.
40 A. Bermingham, op.cit., p.85.
41 M. Tafuri, op. cit., p.82.
42 Le Corbusier, *Toward a New Architecture* (Praeger, New York, 1960), p.9.
43 Carlo Cattaneo, *Scritti economici* (Florence, 1956), pp.4–5, quoted in Aldo Rossi, *The Architecture of the City* (The MIT Press, 1982), p.34.
44 Ralph Waldo Emerson, *Nature I*, quoted in James Turner, *The Politics of Landscape* (Harvard University Press, 1979), p.195.
45 See Lionello Puppi, "The Villa Gardens of the Veneto," *The Italian Garden* (Dumbarton Oaks, 1972), pp. 84–99.
46 Le Corbusier, op. cit., p. 232.
47 Ibid., p. 233.
48 Ibid., p. 68.
49 John R. Stilgoe, *Common Landscape of America, 1580 to 1845* (Yale University Press, 1982), p.14.
50 Anne Verney-Moudon, *Elements of Urban Form*, (manuscript in progress, 1987).
51 See D. R. Coffin, *The Villa in the Life of Renaissance Rome* (Princeton University Press, 1979), p.16.
52 John Ruskin, *Modern Painters* (1843), Vol 3, p.246, quoted in J.B. Jackson, *Discovering the Vernacular Landscape* (Yale University Press, 1984), p. 52.
53 Le Corbusier, *The City of Tomorrow* (Architectural Press, London), p.287, quoted by Tafuri, op.cit., p.48.
54 A. Rossi, *The Architecture of the City* (Cambridge, The MIT Press, 1982), p.126.
55 G. M. Trevelyan, *The Historical Causes of the Present State of Affairs in Italy* (Norton & Co., London, 1923), p. 5.
56 C. Norberg-Schultz *Genius Loci: Towards a Phenomenology of Architecture* (Rizzoli, New York, 1979), p.176.
57 Spiro Kostof, *A History of Architecture* (Oxford University Press, 1985), p.532.
58 D. Wiebenson, op.cit., pp.118–9.
59 Willilam Carlos Williams, *In the American Grain*, p. 108, quoted in David Wyatt, *The fall into Eden* (Cambridge University Press, 1968), p.16.
60 H. B. Johnson, *Order Upon the Land* (Oxford University Press, 1976), p.21.
61 James E. Vance, *This Scene of Man* (Harper's College Press, New York, 1977), p.45, quoted by Paul Groth, "Streetgrids as Frameworks for Urban Variety," *Harvard Architectural Review* (V.2, Spring, 1981) p. 69.
62 Ibid.
63 Henry Nash Smith, *Virgin Land* (Harvard University Press, 1950).
64 See John Reps, *Town Planning in Frontier America* (University of Missouri, 1980).
65 See J. Stilgoe and J. Reps for further information.
66 H.B. Johnson, op.cit., p.28–9.
67 Stilgoe, op.cit., p.103.
68 H.N. Smith, op.cit., 123–4.
69 Robert Riley, "Square to the Road, Hogs to the East," *Places*, Vol.2, No.4, p. 72.
70 Stilgoe, op.cit. p.106–7.
71 Ibid.
72 Anne Verney-Mouton, *Built for Change* (The MIT Press, 1986), p.27.
73 D. Wyatt, op.cit., p.xvi.
74 Ibid.
75 Henry James, *The American Scene* (Bloomington, 1968), p.462, quoted in Kevin Starr *Americans & the California Dream* (Oxford University Press, 1973), p. 418.
76 Le Corbusier, op.cit. p.89.
77 Ibid. p.103.

Identification and credits for small photographs and drawings (those not credited by author):

1. Entrance *allée* to Villa Mondragone, Frascati.
2. The Park at Sceaux.
3. The lake at Stourhead.
4. Oak Hill Farm, Sonoma. (J. Schmidlin).
5. Sheet of water, *Fontana Paolina*, Rome.
6. Vauclause, Provence. (J. Schmidlin).
7. The Chateau at Anet.
8. Detail: *4e. Vue du Parc Français*, Isle of Poplars, Ermenonville. (F. Gébhardt del lith. de Chéyère. Bibliothéque Nationale, Paris).
9. The Château at Dampierre.
10. Olive tree at Wurster Hall, Berkeley.
11. Palazzo Rossi, Pontecchio.
12. Grand stairway, Château at Chantilly.
13. Tempietto Barbaro, Maser.
14. Galleria Vittorio Emanuele II, Milan.
15. Grand stairway, Versailles.
16. Exedra, Chateau at Anet. (J. Schmidlin).
17. Piazza del Popolo, Rome.
18. Entrance allée to Stowe.
19. Canal at Trieste.
20. The Park at Sceaux.
21. Villa Badoer, Fratta Polesine.
22. Detail: *Ville di delizia, o siano palaggi camparecci nello stato di Milano*. (Dumbarton Oaks, Trustees for Harvard University).
23. View toward the grotto, Vaux-le-Vicomte, Melun.
24. The Park at Sceaux.
25. Island/water garden, Villa Lante, Bagnaia.
26. Chateau wall at Lunéville.
27. Ducal Palace wall at Mantua.
28. Trellis gateway at Chantilly. (Bibliothéque Nationale, Paris).
29. Christ Church College, Oxford.
30. Boboli Gardens, Florence.
31. The Park at Sceaux.
32. Detail: *Denkmäler des Theaters. 1–12 Mappe. Mappe 7, Theater und Garten.* (Dumbarton Oaks, Trustees for Harvard University).
33. Villa Badoer, Fratta Polesine.
34. Place Royale, Paris.
35. The Park at Sceaux.
36. Luxembourg Gardens, Paris.
37. Fountains Abbey and Studley Royal, Yorkshire. (J. Schmidlin).
38. Half Moon Pond, Studley Royal, Yorkshire. (J. Schmidlin).
39. Detail: Plan of Garden of St. Leu-Taverny. (Bibliothéque Nationale, Paris).
40. *Plan du rocher et de la grande cascade de St. Leu*. (Bibliothéque Nationale, Paris).
41. Serpentine stream in the English garden at Rambouillet.
42. Detail: *Villas of the Ancients Illustrated*. (Robert Castell; Dumbarton Oaks. Trustees for Harvard University).
43. The Temple of Philosophy at Ermenonville.
44. The Temple of Ancient Virtue at Stowe.
45. The Rotunda at Stowe. (J. Schmidlin).
46. The Temple of Apollo at Stourhead. (J. Schmidlin).
47. Detail: View across the lake at Ermenonville. (Lithograph de Bove; Bibliothéque Nationale, Paris).
48. Detail: Bride's Hall (Mantegna; Ducal Palace, Mantova).
49. Detail: Bride's Hall (Mantegna; Ducal Palace, Mantova).
50. The grotto, Stourhead, Mere.
51. The hut of J.J. Rousseau, Ermenonville. (Thiénol Pinx et Lith.; Bibliothéque Nationale, Paris).
52. Detail: Isle of Poplars (Bibliothéque National, Paris).
53. Cascade, Ermenonville.
54. Detail: *Vue intérieure d'un jardin Anglois*: Moulin Joli. (Daubigny; Bibliothéque Nationale, Paris).
55. The garden at Caserta.
56. Chinoiserie at Parc Monceau, Paris.
57. Detail: *Le Dejeuner de Jambon*. (Lancet; Condé Museum, Chantilly).
58. View from Castle Howard.
59. Pyramid, Parc Monceau, Paris. (J. Schmidlin).
60. The Palladian Bridge, Stowe.
61. Column base at Stowe.
62. The Alpes.
63. Detail: Fireworks at Versailles. (M. Dosso; Bibliothéque Nationale, Paris).
64. Detail: Grotto of stalactites, Parc Monceau, Paris. (Bibliothéque Nationale, Paris).
65. Detail: *Denkmäler des Theaters. 1–12 Mappe, Mappe 7, Theater und Garten*. (Dumbarton Oaks, Trustees for Harvard University).
66. Detail: *Camera degli Sposi* (Mantegna; Ducal Palace, Mantova.)
67. Italian ruin decorated with gothic window to resemble English ruin. (Castello di Brazzá, Santa Margherita, Udine).
68. St. Helena, Napa Valley.
69. Vineyards in Alsace. (J. Schmidlin).
70. Boboli Gardens, Florence.
71. Vauclause, Provence.
72. Route Nationale No.28.
73. "Le lavorazioni e sistemazioni a rittochino (A),
74. a cavalcapoggio (B),
75. a tagliapoggio a superficie unita (C),
76. o divisa in ciglioni (D), da una tavola del *Dizionario di agricoltura* del Gera." (Emilio Sereni, *Storia del paesaggio agrario*

italiano Editori Laterza, Roma-Bari 1984, p. 223).
77 Vauclause, Provence.
78 Vauclause, Provence. (J. Schmidlin).
79 Farm in Po Valley.
80 Urban park, Harrogate, Yorkshire.
81 Field in Normandy.
82 Villa Badoer, Fratta Polesine.
83 Vineyard near Draguignan. (J. Schmidlin).
84 Detail: *Ville di delizia, o siano palaggi camparecci nello stato de Milano*. (Dumbarton Oaks, Trustees for Harvard University).
85 Field near Anet.
86 Farm near Lodi. (J. Schmidlin).
87 Farm near Anet.
88 Tempietto Barbaro, Maser.
89 Flower fields at Lompoc.
90 Farm in Chianti.
91 Service building at Rousham.
92 Canal in Bourgogne.
93 Canal at Dampierre.
94 Canal at Palazzo Rossi.
95 Allée in Sonoma.
96 The park at Sceaux.
97 Temple of Piety, Studley Royal, Yorkshire. (J. Schmidlin).
98 Pantheon, Stourhead, Mere. (J. Schmidlin).
99 Serpentine path at Stourhead. (J. Schmidlin).
100 Grotto at Stourhead.
101 Island at Stourhead. (J. Schmidlin).
102 Mausoleum at Castle Howard.
103 The Temple of Four Winds at Castle Howard.
104 Balustrade between formal garden and fields.
105 Gateway to fields.
106 View south to pyramid in fields.
107 Flower fields at Lompoc.
108 Detail: Bride's Hall (Mantegna; Ducal Palace, Mantova).
109 The Park at Sceaux. (J. Schmidlin).
110 Grand bridge, island, and lake at Blenheim park. (J. Schmidlin).
111 Detail: Castell, *Villas of the Ancients*. (Dumbarton Oaks, Trustees for Harvard University).
112 Farm near Greve, Chianti.
113 Garden rug; Persia, seventeenth century. (Monique Mosser, *Les Jardins*, Paris, 1980, p. 16).
114 Garden plan; Batty Lanley, New *Principles of Gardening* (1728). (Monique Mosser, *Les Jardins*, Paris, 1980, p.40).
115 The green rectangle in Manhattan.
116 Detail: *La Laguna Gelata*. (*Maniera del Guardi*, Cà Rezzonico, Venice).
117 Detail: Tomb of Jean-Jacques Rousseau; Isle of Poplars, Ermenonville. (Engraving by J.M. Moreau. Bibliothéque Nationale, Paris).
118 Detail: Island at Park Buttes Chaumont, Paris. (Bibliothéque Nationale, Paris).
119 Detail: Vue intérieure d'un jardin Anglois: Moulin Joli. (Daubigny; Bibliothéque Nationale, Paris).
120 Island off Albenga.
121 The satyric scene, from Serlio, *Tutte l'opere dell'architettura*, Book II.
122 Detail: *Villas of the Ancients Illustrated*. (Robert Castell; Dumbarton Oaks. Trustees for Harvard University).
123 Tree in park at Sceaux.
124 Tree in Oxfordshire.
125 Grotto at Ermenonville.
126 Dairy at Rombouillet.
127 Detail: *Villas of the Ancients Illustrated*. (Robert Castell; Dumbarton Oaks. Trustees for Harvard University).
128 Serpentine stream in English garden at Rambouillet.
129 Farm near Udine.
130 Farm at Maser.
131 Poplars at Sceaux.
132 Meadow in Tuscany.
133 Farm near Bologna.
134 Canal near Grasse.
135 Road in Gloucestershire.
136 Villa at Asolo.
137 View of Florence from the Boboli Gardens.
138 Allée at the Tuileries. (J. Schmidlin).
139 Canal at Rambouillet.
140 Rectangle of trees around a field in Normandy.
141 Meadow at Nolzay.
142 The Long Walk at Rousham. (J. Schmidlin).
143 The ice house at Désert de Retz. (J. Schmidlin).
144 The Doric Arch at Stowe.
145 Tree at Sceaux.
146 Route into Roccabianca, Emilia-Romagna.
147 Poplars at Sceaux.
148 Via Parione, Rome.
149 Vaux-le-Vicomte.
150 The Gate House at Castle Howard.
151 Black Point Road, Marin County.
152 Trees near Sonoma.
153 Almond orchard in Dixon, California. (Gregory Baird).
154 Street trees in Santa Monica.
155 Street trees in Beverly Hills.
156 House in St. Helena.
157 *Allée* to turkey farm in Sonoma.
158 Vineyards of Napa Valley.
159 *Allée* at Chabot Ranch, St. Helena.
160 The Marina Green, San Francisco.
161 Along Autostrada A1 between Milan and Lodi.
162 The Portico of San Luca, Bologna.
163 Place Royale, Paris.
164 Urban park.
165 Aerial view of Pacific Heights, San Francisco.
166 Plan of the Presidio of San Francisco, California: 1820. (Courtesy, The Bancroft Library).
167 Steep streets become parks.
168 When streets become waterfalls.

Drawing on front cover: *Verneuil*.

Collage on back cover: *Building in Friuli; fields in Lompoc*.